Preaching and Music

"Preachers have always known the deep connections between preaching and music, but for Williams, this partnership results in reciprocal homiletical possibilities of symphonic heights. That music can lighten the preacher's load by sharing in the proclamation of the good news of God is just the pastoral and spiritual promise every preacher needs to hear."

—**KAROLINE M. LEWIS**, Marbury E. Anderson Chair in Biblical Preaching, Luther Seminary, St. Paul, Minnesota

"Preachers with musical training have long intuited the resonance between these two identities, but it is rare to find a book that takes both callings seriously. In *Preaching and Music*, Catherine Williams offers a unique perspective on the multiple connections between preaching and music, inviting preachers and musicians to fully embrace each other as partners in the work of proclamation. This is a joyful book, reminding us of all the ways word and song belong together."

—**ANGELA DIENHART HANCOCK**, Howard C. Scharfe Associate Professor of Homiletics, Pittsburgh Theological Seminary

"In this volume Williams draws upon established homiletical and liturgical voices, but then pulls these to the margins where they can be put into conversation with traditions that have been largely ignored or even disparaged, particularly those of Black and Pentecostal churches. This is not a zero-sum game. Williams demonstrates that when we dismantle the walls that divide our traditions and our roles as preachers and musicians, all can better flourish."

—**MARTIN TEL**, C. F. Seabrook Director of Music, Princeton Theological Seminary

"Catherine Williams takes the global church into the practice rooms of spoken and sung word with a first of its kind homiletics textbook and demonstrates how 'singing can preach and preaching can sing.' With glossary and index, she introduces her integrative musico-homiletical method and also invites readers into the fascinating soundscape of African American preaching. Without romanticized intent, she shows how Africana music and homiletical practices transcend the theoretical codes and categories developed by Europeans, underscoring how cultural experiences involving music and proclamation reflect the Holy Spirit's indifference to binaries which suggest that life is divisible in God's world. *Preaching and Music* strikes the right chord and hits the right note!"

—**KENYATTA R. GILBERT**, dean and professor of homiletics, Howard University School of Divinity

"In this wise and inspiring book, Williams—herself a pastor-preacher, as well as preaching professor and trained musicologist—invites preachers and church musicians to be creative allies, planning every worship service as a deliberate interweaving of sermon and song, guided by a clearly focused message. Chapter by chapter, we learn accessible strategies for creating a synergistic relationship between music and spoken word, enlisting preacher and worshipers as co-proclaimers of gospel news. Especially rich is Williams's exploration of Africana worship traditions, where proclamation arises amid a soundscape of Spirit-energized dialogue between pulpit and pew. This is a book congregations must gift to each of their preachers, lay worship leaders, and musicians."

—**SALLY A. BROWN**, Elizabeth M. Engle Professor Emerita, Princeton Theological Seminary

Preaching and Music

Powerful Partners in Proclamation

Catherine E. Williams

Foreword by Luke A. Powery

CASCADE *Books* • Eugene, Oregon

PREACHING AND MUSIC
Powerful Partners in Proclamation

Copyright © 2025 Catherine E. Williams. All rights reserved. Except for brief quotations in critical publications or reviews, no part of this book may be reproduced in any manner without prior written permission from the publisher. Write: Permissions, Wipf and Stock Publishers, 199 W. 8th Ave., Suite 3, Eugene, OR 97401.

Cascade Books
An Imprint of Wipf and Stock Publishers
199 W. 8th Ave., Suite 3
Eugene, OR 97401

www.wipfandstock.com

PAPERBACK ISBN: 978-1-6667-1423-4
HARDCOVER ISBN: 978-1-6667-1424-1
EBOOK ISBN: 978-1-6667-1425-8

Cataloguing-in-Publication data:

Names: Williams, Catherine E., author. | Powery, Luke A., 1974–, foreword.

Title: Preaching and music : powerful partners in proclamation / Catherine E. Williams ; foreword by Luke A. Powery.

Description: Eugene, OR : Cascade Books, 2025 | Includes bibliographical references and index(es).

Identifiers: ISBN 978-1-6667-1423-4 (paperback) | ISBN 978-1-6667-1424-1 (hardcover) | ISBN 978-1-6667-1425-8 (ebook)

Subjects: LCSH: Preaching. | Music and language. | Music in churches.

Classification: BV4211.2 .W49 2025 (paperback) | BV4211.2 .W49 (ebook)

VERSION NUMBER 03/24/25

Scripture quotations, unless otherwise noted, are from the New Revised Standard Version of the Bible Updated Edition, copyright © 2023 by the Division of Christian Education of the National Council of the Churches of Christ in the U.S.A. and are used by permission.

"I Go to Sing," copyright © 2019 Lindy Thompson. All rights reserved. Used by permission.

"Restless Weaver," copyright © 1995 Chalice Press. All rights reserved. Used by permission.

"When Memory Fades," copyright © 2002 GIA Publications, Inc. All rights reserved. Used by permission.

Contents

Foreword by Luke A. Powery | vii
Acknowledgments | xi
Introduction | xiii

1. Liturgical Integrity | 1
2. Framing the Sermon | 27
3. Musicality and Black Preaching | 50
4. Preaching and Music as Spiritual Care | 86
5. Hymn Exegesis | 118

Epilogue | 129
Appendix | 131
Bibliography | 133
Subject Index | 141
Scripture Index | 145
Song Title Index | 147

Foreword
LUKE A. POWERY

CHRISTIAN PREACHERS HAVE OFTEN suffered from a myopic vision about the genres of proclamation. At least in the logocentric Protestant tradition, there is a misguided proclivity to only emphasize pulpit speech as vital to proclaiming the gospel. Of course, there is the faithful affirmation and stress on "the Word," a Word that was "in the beginning . . . and . . . with God, and . . . was God" (John 1:1). Yet what is often muted, as it relates to homiletical theory and practice in both the academy and the church, is that "the Word became flesh" (John 1:14). This means that just as God's Word became flesh to proclaim the Word beyond words, preaching Jesus Christ requires more than verbal articulation. It calls for enfleshment or embodiment. It calls for a holistic approach. For this Word to "live among us" as human flesh means it breathes, it walks, it moves, it dances, it sounds—it even sings! If we proclaim the Word through speech alone, this is not the fully incarnate Word of God.

There is theo-biblical precedent for this. In the Old Testament, Zephaniah 3:17–18a reads:

> The Lord, your God, is in your midst,
>   a warrior who gives victory;

> he will rejoice over you with gladness;
>   he will renew you in his love;
> he will exult over you with loud singing
>   as on a day of festival.

Typically, we affirm that God speaks, *Deus dixit*; this is not unusual. But seldom, if ever, do we hear and emphasize that God sings! *Deus cantat*. In this prophetic literature, God sings loudly over a people with joy. To convey a message, God sometimes sings. The divine intones. God's word, in this case, is music. Moreover, these words about God singing are a part of a larger portion of scripture in Zephaniah that is actually the genre of song (3:14–20). The prophet writes a song that tells of God singing—a double accent on the possibility of song as proclamation.

Catherine Williams offers us all a homiletical gift when she highlights the legacy of Scripture that blends proclamation and song with particular reference to the hymnic fragments all throughout the Bible. Zephaniah 3:14–20 is but one example. There are many others. Miriam sings (Exodus 15:20–21). Hannah sings (1 Samuel 1:1–10). Mary sings (Luke 1:46–55). The elders, living creatures, and angels sing (Revelation 5:8–13). To be clear, however, their songs are not mere musical entertainment, they are proclamation. They tell the story of God and God's people in melody and rhythm. In our time, too often the fullness of gospel proclamation is squeezed into principles or points, which misses the actual nature of the gospel as an enfleshed Word. As Walter Brueggemann has noted, a "prose-flattened"[1] gospel is insufficient for Christian proclamation. The gospel is not a plethora of intellectual points, rather it is the story of God in Jesus Christ, a story proclaimed in our canon of Scripture through diverse genres—narrative, history, proverbs, epistles, poetry, hymns, and more.

It is almost as if Williams is declaring in relation to preaching, "Finally comes the singer!" She challenges us to be more "whole" preachers, true to a gospel story about an embodied God. A snapshot of this gospel in Philippians 2:5–11 is strikingly told in the form of a hymn known as "the Christ hymn."

---

1. Brueggemann, *Finally Comes the Poet*, 1.

Foreword

> Christ Jesus,
> who, though he existed in the form of God,
> > did not regard equality with God
> > as something to be grasped,
> but emptied himself,
> > taking the form of a slave,
> > assuming human likeness.
> And being found in appearance as a human,
> > he humbled himself
> > and became obedient to the point of death—
> > even death on a cross.
> Therefore God exalted him. . . .

The Apostle Paul proclaims the gospel—the compelling story of God in Christ—not merely with words but in a song. Williams liberates preachers from limiting the word of God through their preaching by only approaching it in one way when "the wideness of God's mercy"[2] calls us to widen our homiletical repertoire.

Not only is there theo-biblical precedence for this beautiful partnership between preaching and music, but within liturgies, this homiletical tag team has been working together in practice for centuries. Williams illuminates how preaching and music have been collaborating for proclamation in congregations for years. Her writing is a loving revelation, an insightful uncovering of what has been and what could be, theologically, culturally, and practically. From an entire service as proclamation to hymns framing sermons to the musicality of Black preaching to preaching and music as resources for spiritual care to hymn exegesis, she reveals the multiplicity of ways "preaching and music [are] conjoined." She presents variations on this theme to reveal a rich and more robust homiletical method.

The generative and intimate relationship between preaching and music goes a step further as expressed by gospel singer and pastor Shirley Caesar who once said in an interview, "I sing my sermons and I preach my songs."[3] This symbiotic practice aligns with the wisdom of the spirituals. There is no scholarly certitude

---

2. Faber, "There's a Wideness in God's Mercy," 121.
3. Gilkes, "Shirley Caesar," 12–16.

Foreword

about whether these spiritual songs came first and led to sermons, or whether sermons did and led to the songs. But this is the critical point spirituals make. Both singing and speaking can proclaim the gospel! Williams reveals this deep intertwining of preaching and music well. It is, as she calls it, an "integrative delight."

Rather than pit the sermon against the song or vice versa, she aims for reconciliation, a seamless symbiosis between preaching and music, even pastor and musician. Williams enfleshes another way other than the so-called "worship wars" of old. She sees a "wonder-working power"[4] at play between preaching and music for the glorious worship of God and the faithful proclamation of the Word. She resists the disjoining of sermon and song. She refuses to give in to this easy bifurcation but yearns for a holistic "word made flesh" or even a "word made music." She knows, as any humble, honest, and wise preacher can attest, that on any given Sunday, people may receive more from music sung or heard than from the spoken sermon.

Williams has a whole and holy, symphonic vision that synergizes homiletics, musicology, and liturgiology, a triad so often explored in silos. Her integrative or reconciling practical theological scholarship is a gift for the church and academy, the choir guild and the research guild. In her scholarship, the twain shall meet, and when they meet, there is heavenly music from the Maker, intoning a fresh word of God among us.

This engaging volume is a call to attune our ears, minds, hearts, and homiletical practices with the "tuning fork of the Spirit." When this occurs, anything can happen in the pulpit because the fiery Wind is free. If the unknown black bards were right, then we'll even "sing when the Spirit says-a sing." There's so much resonance from engaging this melodious book, that the only proper response is to find our way into sounding out the glory of God. If God sings to proclaim the Word, so should we! With this hymnic homiletic in mind, we are left to ponder, "How can [we] keep from singing?"[5]

---

4. Jones, "There Is Power in the Blood," 258.
5. Anon., "How Can I Keep From Singing."

Acknowledgments

THIS BOOK OWES ITS life, from conception to delivery, to an entire village of people who preach, teach, sing, pray, and love. Deep gratitude goes to the musicians, preachers, and liturgical practitioners who took time to have generative conversations with me, some of whose thoughts have made their way into this work: Jan Ammon, Melvin Baber, Mary Alice Birdwhistell, Randall Bradley, Andrea Brown, Kathy Collier, Jane Dutton, Liz Fulmer, Mike Greaves, Manny Hampton, Genevieve Karki, Quentin Lawson, Jana Purkis-Brash, John Smith, Martin Tel, Joe Torres, and Kellie Turner.

I could hardly ask for more collegial theological sounding boards than my colleagues at Lancaster Theological Seminary: Lee Barrett, Greg Carey, Myka Kennedy-Stephens, Vanessa Lovelace, Julia O'Brien, Darryl Stevens, and Anne Thayer, all of whom read and provided gracious, scholarly feedback on some aspect of this writing. I am grateful for the love and patience of my students at Lancaster Theological Seminary and Lexington Theological Seminary, who heard these lectures and whose feedback and ideas refined my original thoughts. Special thanks to Cam Richesson

Acknowledgments

for her research help. Homiletical colleagues graciously came alongside me during this work, offering feedback and suggesting resources: Sally Brown, Cleophus LaRue, and Frank Thomas.

Thanks to Jeron Ashford and Frank Gray, writing experts who guided me as the manuscript developed. And as I persevered through the years of writing, it was AnneMarie Mingo and my Sister Scholars who inspired me and kept me accountable for hours on end as we wrote together on Zoom every second Saturday of the month and during the summer Wednesday writing meetings. Thanks to all who prayed with me through the four-year writing process; your prayers were my lifeline on more days than you would imagine.

My musical family deserves special mention. My father, and first pastor, the late Rev. Dr. William Patrick Ryan, and my mother, the late Miriam Rose Ryan, created the foundation for this project when they nurtured my musical gifts within the context of the church. My siblings, Gwendolyn Smith, Theodore (Ted) Ryan, Rhoda Ryan, and Donald Ryan, have each inspired my musical growth by their solid example. My musical children, Harran Jesse and Joanna Elizabeth, have been tireless cheerleaders; thank you both so much! And to my devoted husband, Harran, there is simply no repaying you for your patience, personal sacrifice, prayers, and love that have been a bedrock of support throughout this writing. My ultimate thanks goes to my Creator, Redeemer, and Sustainer, without whom there would be no good news to proclaim through the powerful partnership of sermon and song. *Soli Deo Gloria.*

Introduction

THE POPULAR BALLAD "THE Prayer" skyrocketed to fame in 1999, thanks to the singing duo of Andrea Bocelli and Celine Dion. We cannot help but sense the power of each singer's talent in the dramatic solo vocals. But when we hear them as a duo, whether crooning in harmony over each other or belting call-and-response phrases in English and Italian, the multiplied effect is riveting. This coupling of two magnificent voices, this integrative delight, invites our hearts to soar as we listen to this sung prayer.

As a musically trained homiletician, I find similar integrative delight when sermon and song are richly blended in worship. Legendary tensions between preachers and church musicians notwithstanding, many congregants experience this uplifting integration and synergy in Christian worship services across denominational and cultural lines every Sunday, somewhere in the world. This book takes the reader, whether student or practitioner, through a number of ways this blended method plays out effectively in worship. In conversation with liturgical, homiletical, theological, and musical partners, I examine several services and sermons that

Introduction

make the case for effective blending of preaching and music in one variation or another. Preachers who consider themselves unmusical will discover practical, accessible ways to make sermons more participatory and therefore more memorable, appealing to both head and heart. And most critically for some readers, each chapter has talking points for generating fruitful conversations between pastors and musicians.

While other writers have published volumes whose titles and/or content invite reflection on the relationship between preaching and music, *Preaching and Music* presents this dyad as a homiletical method with preacher and musician as proclamatory partners. It explores what happens when the preacher integrates music and preaching in a variety of ways, drawing both preacher and church musician into this act of proclamation. It claims intentional blending of sermon and song as a homiletical method with historical roots and contemporary appeal. This method invites musical preachers to bring their full selves to their homiletical art. It also invites preachers who consider themselves unmusical to dip their toes into these waters with just one variation of this proven practice; I have heard preachers who do not sing use this rhetorical partnership in powerful sermons. I foreground this method for the sake of homiletical and liturgical richness in worship, providing guidance and examples that equip and encourage the musically timid or novice preacher. It is also my hope that church musicians, a group in which I claim emerita status, will find this book valuable, as it addresses some of the liturgical issues they may find difficult to articulate in a way that connects with preachers. This book celebrates and validates the contributions church musicians bring to the task of proclamation.

As one who teaches preaching, I write out of a pedagogical concern for sociocultural resonance and justice in the classroom. With all its power and proven effectiveness in congregations everywhere, every Sunday, one question remains as I think about the legacy of homiletics. Why is this powerful, proven method not routinely taught to students of preaching? Students in introductory preaching classes will likely get to know classic approaches such

Introduction

as expository, inductive, narrative, the four-page, and even the three-point sermon. I believe these standalone forms of preaching are all enriched by some variation of this method of blended sermon and song. Students of color are likely to complete standard introductory preaching classes with scant if any reference to an approach that integrates music with the spoken delivery, yet this method is central to preaching in the churches from which many such students have entered seminary, and to which they will one day return. Consequently, this volume is for the preacher and for students of preaching who wish to broaden and strengthen the integrity of their homiletical approaches and who are willing to venture outside their comfort zones.

In a very real sense this book is an extension of my own professional identity. Thanks to lifelong experiences that span several Protestant traditions, I find myself at the nexus of this engagement between liturgy, theology, homiletics, and musicology. I was born into the family of a pastor-musician in Trinidad and Tobago, a Caribbean nation made famous for giving the world the musical delights of calypso and steelpan. My decades of formal musical training and experience as a pianist, vocalist, vocal coach, choral conductor, and church music director all happened within close range of Christian communities in the Caribbean and North America. Pentecostal, Anglican, Presbyterian, Baptist, Lutheran, Methodist, and nondenominational influences have each planted milestone markers on my spiritual journey and professional identity. More than two decades of training and experience as a homilist (one who preaches) and homiletician (one who studies and teaches preaching) have provided me abundant opportunities to learn, make mistakes, then learn some more about what makes preaching compelling—how, when, and where. Exposure to a variety of worship liturgies has developed and honed my personal database of hundreds of "psalms, hymns, and spiritual songs"[1] across the many genres sung in Christian worship. Scores of lecture-discussions in preaching and worship classes have connected me

---

1. Common nomenclature for congregational song taken from New Testament writings found in Ephesians 5:19 and Colossians 3:16.

Introduction

with students from various countries, denominations, and cultural backgrounds who have expanded and enriched my homiletical and liturgical horizons. These educational opportunities and faith experiences are inextricably woven into my identity as a practical theologian; hence my passion for this blend of preaching and singing, and my claim for its value to the field of homiletics.

I use the terms hymn, song, music, congregational song, and singing interchangeably to indicate sung lyrics in the context of worship. Within the scope of this book, I do not differentiate between homily and sermon, though in other contexts differentiation between the two is warranted. Sermon, homily, preaching, and proclamation appear interchangeably, and in some cases may depend on the preferred term of a particular preacher or congregation. Preaching and its synonyms are the act of declaring or telling forth the call, comfort, and challenge of the Gospel in a service of public Christian worship.

While we may not pinpoint its origins with precision, there is evidence in early biblical writings that this musico-homiletical method was employed. Preaching looked different then than now, but the notion of proclaiming the Word of the Lord, of bearing public witness to God's work, is at least as old as the songs attributed to Moses and Miriam in Exodus 15. The Hebrew Bible also gives us the book of Psalms, poetry that was chanted in Hebrew worship. These lyrical gems have been called mini sermons, on account of the ways they proclaim the good news of God to God's people and beyond.[2]

In the collection of New Testament writings, we find writers breaking forth into song in their letters. The writings of Paul, the epistle to the Hebrews, and the letters attributed to Peter, James, and John all contain fragments of or allusions to the Hebrew psalter or prophetic hymns, as the writers combine teaching or preaching with song. We also find New Testament writers inserting fragments of early Christian hymns or Greek poetry in their letters.[3] We can only imagine how this artistic texture and lyri-

---

2. Borger, Tel, and Witvliet, "Introduction," in *Psalms for All Seasons*, ii.

3. Philippians 2:6–11 is an example of a Christ hymn, while Acts 17:27–28 is a fragment of Greek poetry.

Introduction

cal color may have kept listeners engaged throughout what may otherwise have been monochromatic monologue. We are indebted to a legacy of biblical precedent for this pattern of blending proclamation and song.

In the history of the Christian church, we read of several notable practitioners of this homiletical dyad. Prominent figures who have combined sermon and song with enduring impact include the German preacher, Martin Luther (1483–1546). Luther and his protegees not only used hymns as illustrations in their sermons but would often use Luther's scripturally and theologically dense hymns in lieu of biblical texts. Lutheran scholar Robert A. Kolb concludes that "Luther's concept of God's Word as the Holy Spirit's instrument for bringing people to saving faith enabled his followers to see in hymn texts a basis from which the biblical message could be proclaimed."[4] In some Lutheran congregations today preaching on hymn texts remains a beloved homiletical practice, and the criteria for selecting such a hymn comply with historically strict theological and doctrinal standards.[5]

Historical exemplars of this method also include Charles Wesley (1707–78), arguably the most prolific example. Although known best for his thousands of contributions to Christian hymnody, very early in the development of the Methodist movement Charles established himself as "a preacher of significant ability whose discourses were powerful and able to affect those to whom they were addressed."[6] Charles's hymns and homilies had a remarkable impact on early Methodism. He would often preach and sing on the same text. Historian J. Ernest Rattenbury believes it was Charles's preaching and not his brother John's "that was the most effective and comprehensive statement of Methodist doctrine. He expressed in attractive and forceful verse what sometimes John wrote in labored syllogisms."[7] Preachers have since found Charles Wesley's biblically grounded lyrics a robust complement to and

4. Kolb, "Preaching on Luther's Hymn Texts," 17.
5. Bombardo, "When All Else Fails, Preach a Hymn."
6. Newport, *Sermons of Charles Wesley*, 4.
7. Rattenbury, *Evangelical Doctrines*, 61.

Introduction

inspiration for their homilies. Later historical precedents for the synergy of preaching and song are found in the revivalist preaching of the Great Awakening, the North American camp meetings, and the evangelistic crusades of proclamation partners such as D. L. Moody and Ira D. Sankey.

The history of African Americans has also charted a course for this practice of music-infused preaching, particularly in that invisible institution of slave religion which birthed the spirituals. These songs of the spirit were often a natural outgrowth of preaching, composed communally as gathered worshipers synthesized and recounted their understanding of the Scriptures. Homiletician Luke Powery believes the spirituals can teach preachers how to preach hope amid death, a meaningful idea in our pandemic- and war-troubled era where death has intruded incorrigibly into our lives. In the African American tradition, preaching can sing just as well as songs can preach: "Singing the spirituals was a part of what it meant to preach; thus even singing the spirituals counted as preaching. . . . The most profound sign of their union is the musicality of both."[8] Black preaching continues to organically generate music in, for, and through the sermon.

Sermon and song have found synergy theologically, historically, and culturally. I have also looked to musicology for a technical lens through which to view this dynamic partnership. Theme and variations is a musical form where the composer begins the piece with a basic, often simple melodic idea or pattern—the theme. The beauty of the completed work lies in the ways the composer embellishes this theme, creating musically distinct variations of it, in much the way a phone camera might create different versions of a single photo, playing with color or light. In the theme and variations musical form, the composer rearranges the melody, reorders the notes, changes the rhythm or timing, and plays with harmony, all while creating a variety of sounds and effects built upon the original, always-recognizable theme.

Based on this model, preaching and music conjoined is the basic theme or practice on which this book builds. The variations

8. Powery, *Dem Dry Bones*, 23.

Introduction

or ways this joining can happen are countless, depending on the imagination of the preacher, the aptitude of the congregation, and the promptings of the Holy Spirit. Of these possible variations I take a close look at five, one in each of the following chapters. Each chapter contains at least one sermon or service which illustrates the variation being explored. Each chapter also ends with notes meant to generate theological and musical conversations between the preacher and the church musician.

Chapter 1 examines purposeful alignment of the sermon with the music sung or played from beginning to end in the worship service, toward the goal of liturgical integrity. This variation comes together best through advance worship planning by a team of two or more that includes the preacher. As the weight of proclamation is distributed throughout the liturgy, it gives preachers more latitude to sharpen the sermon's focus, allowing the music to proclaim the preacher's major and supporting ideas—the sermon does not need to say it all. The collaborative work of the preacher and musician creates coherence between service elements, providing a richer experience for the worshiper.

Chapter 2 looks at the music that frames or bookends the sermon, whether sung by congregation, soloist, or choir. Before the sermon, the hymn of preparation, or sermonic selection as it is sometimes called, serves to set the tone of the sermon, foreshadowing the sermon's focus or main idea. In some traditions this hymn has an invocational role; its purpose is to call upon and establish the presence of the Spirit to bring to life the preached word. Following the sermon a hymn of response or invitation gives the congregation opportunity to answer the call, question, or challenge of the sermon. This chapter contains a reflection on the liturgical practice known as the altar call. Dismissed by some traditions, the altar call remains a time-honored practice in others, providing a space for a musically underscored encounter with the divine. Conversation between preacher and musician centers on how to best effect those bridge-building moments leading into and out of the sermon.

Introduction

Chapter 3 discusses the homiletical musicality of African American sermons and songs. In this discussion we are invited to broaden our understanding regarding what counts as music. The function of musicality in and around a Black sermon is often a culturally nuanced blend of variations of our theme as explored in other chapters. The homiletical concept of attunement is introduced in this chapter as a lens through which to view the Black sermon from its conception to its close. The chapter provides a musico-homiletical glossary of terms that aim to explain the correlation between musicology and homiletics in African-American preaching. And since singing can preach as convincingly as preaching can sing in Black church traditions, this chapter features an analysis of two sermonic examples and one gospel music Tiny Desk concert.

The fourth chapter in this volume is a response to the need for soul care in our congregations, devastated as they are by pandemic deaths, denominational shrinkages, armed global conflicts, social upheavals, and partisan polarization. In this variation of our basic theme, we take our cue from the psalmists who understand and model how corporate lament and proclaiming God's faithfulness can happen jointly. Preaching that tends to hearts is informed by trauma specialists whose work indicates the need for complex, communal approaches to restoration. Singing and proclaiming together is a source of individual and communal healing. The conversation between preacher and church musician in this chapter seeks to discover how preaching and music may be more psalmlike in form and content.

In chapter 5 we look at hymn exegesis. We learn how to do a close reading and analysis of a hymn text similarly to how we would exegete a biblical passage in preparation for preaching on it. This exercise assumes a hymn worthy of such examination, which takes biographical, occasional, historical, theological, literary, musical, and homiletical perspectives into account. The conversation between pastor and musician centers around services entirely devoted to the singing of hymns.

Introduction

This book was conceived in the midst of death. When I began writing, a global pandemic was in full swing, casting a pall of devastation and despair over most of the world as we faced the largest incidence of mass death in our lifetimes. Scores of armed conflicts on every major continent continue to generate fears of a pending war that entangles major global powers. Democracy is in peril in countries where it once flourished. Tragic violence of all kinds flourishes in our homes and on our streets. Amid all the paranoia, panic, and possibilities of our time, preaching, more than ever, is called upon to leverage the good news of God with us and for us. But preaching does not have to bear the weight of such urgent proclamation on its own. Music in all its forms also has the capacity to declare the Word of God for the people of God. Chaplains and pastors know of this mystical power of music at the bedside of someone otherwise unresponsive—a song breaking through the frustrating barrier of cognitive disease, or an old hymn erasing anxious wrinkles from a fevered brow. Music and preaching need each other to apply a much-needed balm to heal our traumatized, sin-sick souls.

I offer what follows with a prayer that music will take her place in and around the pulpit as a trustworthy proclaimer of the Word of God.

1

Liturgical Integrity

PREACHING IS AN ACT of worship that takes place within the context of public Christian gatherings. We call these gatherings services of worship and refer to what happens within these services as the liturgy, whether formally or informally put together. To think of preaching as part of our weekly liturgy, it helps to consider the arc of the entire worship service. What would it look and sound like if all we do, from the start to the end of a service, is intentional and purposeful, the guiding purpose being the scripture or theme of the day, around which the liturgy is built? In this chapter I examine liturgical integrity from contrasting angles—what it is and what it is not. Then I invite the reader to expand their understanding of proclamation, to imagine how an entire service might cohere around declaring God's good news. The chapter contains two examples of services designed with intention and care, which we discuss in detail. This leads to a discussion on team-based worship planning that includes ideas and practical resources for solo pastors. The chapter ends with discussion around selected talking points for pastor-musician collaboration.

LITURGY

The word "liturgy" falls naturally off the tongue as some of us speak of what happens in church every Sunday. For others of us the word is fraught with negative associations of perfunctory words and actions. Liturgy at its most basic level is simply the pattern of activities we engage as a people when we meet to worship God together. For most of us this happens every Sunday. Some of us experience a formal liturgy in which each activity is scripted within a precise order or flow. For those of us who might think of our services as nonliturgical, what happens in worship seems more free form. Yet even for those of us who speak of our services as led by the Spirit, there are certain elements that happen every time: welcome or greeting, prayer, singing, an offering, and a sermon. Though informally structured, these acts of worship form our liturgy, and chances are they happen in more or less the same order every Sunday. Liturgy in this chapter refers to both scripted and unscripted services of worship. And I believe the most meaningful experiences of worship carry a sense of integrity.

Liturgical integrity calls for the various parts of the worship service to be well aligned and meaningfully connected. It is what Lisa Allen advocates in her OneWord model, a liturgical design where one message is communicated by all elements of the service.[1] The outcome we are seeking is that worshipers hear the Word of the Lord through musical proclamation that is consistent in its witness and in harmony with the verbal proclamation of the Word through the sermon. In this variation of our theme of conjoined preaching and music the weight of proclamation is spread throughout the service rather than resting squarely on the pulpit.

But first a lesson in contrast. My college conducting professor had a method of teaching us what correct vocal production felt like in our bodies. She would ask us to sing the note or phrase badly on purpose. When we screeched or yelled, ignoring all the vocal training we had been taught, she would ask us to note how that felt in our bodies. Then, carefully coaching us into the more

---

1. Allen, *OneWord Worship Model*, 26.

desirable sound, she would invite us to repeat the note or phrase with more intention, then pause to check how that felt. Her goal was to help our bodies "know" the more purposeful sound using the pedagogical method of contrast.

In keeping with this method, I ask you to imagine with me a poorly aligned worship service at the beginning of the school year with a Christian education emphasis. The theme of this service, "Passing on the Faith," is based on Psalm 78:1–8 where the psalmist records that God "established a testimony in Israel and appointed a law in Israel which he commanded our fathers that they should make them known to their children that the generations to come might know them." Four hymns feature in this service. It opens with "It Is Well with My Soul." Before the sermon, the congregation sings "We Shall Overcome Someday." Following the sermon is the ballad "Let There Be Peace on Earth." The closing hymn is a joyous rendition of "Glory, Glory Hallelujah Since I Laid My Burdens Down." If this sounds like a lack of thematic congruence, that is the point. It feels out of alignment with the theme of passing on the faith to sing of the assurance of peace, the hope of social justice, a prayer for world peace, and a spiritual about laying down one's burdens. While these songs in their own ways are a fine contribution to a worship service, they not only fail to align well with the direction of this service, but they also take us mentally and spiritually in different directions with no suggestion of a journey or purpose.

A service with liturgical integrity, on the other hand, seeks to combine proclamation in speech and song so that the messages proclaimed are harmonious and ultimately give the listener a strong sense of having encountered God in a particular way. A contrasting example of how the music might more effectively proclaim in this service would include any of the following selections or comparable numbers: Isaac Watts's "Let Children Hear the Mighty Deeds,"[2] Greg Scheer's "What We Have Heard, What We Have Known,"[3] or Ruth Duck's "God, We Thank You for

---

2. Watts, "Let Children Hear."
3. Scheer, "People of the Lord," 632.

Our People."[4] Let me be clear that we are not seeking some ideal scenario with strict, seamless, musical adherence to the scripture or theme; such precision can make for a sterile, inorganic experience of worship. There are times when music, particularly opening hymns, may need to do nothing other than offer praise and thanksgiving to God. There are other times when, as my colleague Martin Tel notes, we just need to sing a heart song for the sake of spiritual care.[5] Rather than thematic precision, what liturgical integrity calls for is a sense of intentionality around choosing what the work of the people will look like in coherently proclaiming the message of the day.

A service planned with intention and purpose is one where each element can answer with integrity the question, "Why are we doing this?" This is so whether the service is scripted or freer in form. In my worship classes I press the students, as they design services of worship, to keep the matter of intention before them. Many of them who attend church regularly have become used to a particular format and flow of a worship service. When asked to design one for a class assignment they naturally default to what they have grown accustomed to. When pressed for the significance of each element of their service they often find themselves in that awkward position of verbalizing for the first time something they have been doing for years without really reflecting on it. Much of worship is based on rituals that define us as a community.[6] We become comfortable with our weekly practices, not seeing any need to put them under scrutiny because . . . well, that's just who we are. And because these rituals have pulled us into a communal identity it is easy to believe the underlying assumptions are shared by everyone and our practices need no explanation. Moreover, members of a congregation are prepared to leave matters of liturgical intentionality in the hands of our leaders—an even greater

---

4. Duck, "God, We Thank You," 376.

5. Martin Tel, conversation with author, February 28, 2022.

6. I find Gail Ramshaw's description most useful for what we do in worship when she refers to rituals as "defined actions that are repeated, communal, and symbolic." See Ramshaw, *Christian Worship*, 33.

Liturgical Integrity

reason for pastors, church musicians, or seminary students of worship to do this kind of reflection well. At stake here is the issue of proclamation. What messages are we communicating through the various elements of worship? The importance of this question is tied to the outcomes of our worship liturgies, where everything we do and say communicates—intentionally or unwittingly—some idea about God. Our worship proclaims.

PROCLAMATION

I daresay most Christians or churchgoers consider preaching and proclamation as speech-driven activities.[7] Yet there are liturgical practitioners and scholars who would invite us into a broader understanding of these terms, widening the scope of preaching and proclamation to include many wordless and artistic expressions of worship. While there may be good reason to differentiate between the terms "preaching" and "proclamation," I use them synonymously in this broader sense. As homiletical terms, preaching and proclamation share the task of announcing God's good news. Proclamation in this chapter indicates the act of spreading the good news of God in Christ through any effective means of communication. In that way it is multivalent in its liturgical perspectives. For the perspective of provenance, we turn to homiletician James Kay.

In his "Theology of Proclamation" entry in the *New Interpreter's Handbook of Preaching*, Kay points us to the etymologies—Latin *proclamatio* and Greek *kerysso*—of our English word "proclamation." The original concept indicates messengers, heralds, or sent ones who declare or announce a message originating with a sender of substantial significance. The ancient image of "a herald dispatched ahead of the royal entourage to proclaim the monarch's mandates or to announce the sovereign's imminent arrival"[8] may be a stretch for the contemporary imagination.

---

7. Williams, "Proclamation." This chapter is a revision and expansion of the article.

8. See Kay, "Theology of Proclamation," in Wilson, *New Interpreter's*

However, those of us who preach understand our pulpit speech as making declarations or announcements that originate from a place of greater significance than ourselves. We understand ourselves as heralds of the messages announced or declared in the scriptures. The New Testament kerygma is described in Paul's writings as "euangelion, that is, as 'good news' or 'gospel.'" Such proclamation is significant, timely, even urgent; "it matters for the good of the hearers and for the good of the world."[9] Unfortunately, these historical associations with the word "proclamation" have condensed its meaning and place into the confines of the pulpit.

PRIMACY OF PREACHING

Our Protestant liturgical legacy has predisposed us to hearing this good news proclaimed exclusively or primarily through the reading of scripture and the sermon that follows. This has not always been the case. In her condensed overview of liturgical history, Sally A. Brown traces the pendulum swing from worship where both Word and Table proclaimed God's good news to the extreme where the Table mattered almost exclusively; the Word was given short shrift. Consequently, it was intrinsic to the work of the sixteenth-century reformers to reassert the primacy of the Word in worship. As such, "the ultimate effect of the reformers' efforts was to throw worship out of balance in the other direction. Protestant services of worship became largely preaching events. The effects of this overbalance toward the pulpit instead of the table can still be detected in the worship patterns of many Protestant churches, especially in North America."[10] This pulpit-centric understanding of proclamation closely aligns with preaching traditions in worshiping communities of color.

Melva Costen Wilson corroborates this liturgical shift as she explains the high esteem for the preached word in *African American*

Handbook of Preaching, 493–98.

9. See Kay, "Theology of Proclamation," in Wilson, *New Interpreter's Handbook of Preaching*, 494.

10. Brown and Powery, *Ways of the Word*, 89.

Liturgical Integrity

Christian Worship: "'Is there a word from the Lord?' This question, which was embedded in the souls of the slaves, continues with African American worshipers. For some, all of the other elements are preliminary to the preached word."[11] Similar liturgical values apply in many Hispanic congregations, where preaching is expected at every gathering. Justo González informs us, "Hispanic Protestants have taken the Reformation's emphasis on the preaching of the word to the point that there can hardly be a service—sometimes even those advertised as 'prayer services'—without preaching—or at least a brief homily."[12] It is not unusual in worship gatherings to hear the sermon introduced by a worship leader who announces, "And now we come to the most important part of the service, the preached word!" This value of the primacy of pulpit speech runs deep in Protestant traditions across the spectrum, from mainline to free church. Yet if we examine closely our liturgies, whether scripted or informal, will we not find the good news of the gospel threaded through the fabric of the service?

This broadened understanding of preaching is not new. In his discussion of the reformed understanding of the threefold Word of God, Kay reminds us that preaching is not restricted to pulpit speech: "In its broadest sense preaching is everything the church says and does in proclaiming the gospel. . . . It is the comprehensive proclamation and announcement of the Christian message in word and act."[13] Tom Long echoes this homiletical theology when he reminds us, "The whole church proclaims the gospel, and the preaching of sermons is but one part of this larger ministry. So when a preacher stands in the pulpit, reads the Scripture, and preaches the sermon, this action is but another form of the one common ministry to which the whole church is called."[14]

I can almost hear some readers despairing that, if preaching is everything the church says and does in proclaiming the gospel, doesn't that diminish or dilute the sacred or even professional

---

11. Costen, *African American Christian Worship*, 91.
12. González and Jiménez, *Púlpito*, 59.
13. Kay, *Preaching and Theology*, 17.
14. Long, *Witness of Preaching*, 4.

value of the pulpit? Why go through the trouble at all to study Hebrew and Greek languages, hermeneutics, and biblical criticism? Why bother to take classes in speech and preaching if the sermonic event does not bear the full or primary import of proclaiming the Word of God? My untamed response would be that if human vocality were all God had to count on to make God's Word known, God would be up a creek without a paddle more Sundays than we imperfect messengers would care to acknowledge. My more reasoned response would be to point to the diversity found in divine means of communicating with us humans. We have a theological model that invites us into a wider view of our work as proclaimers.

If our work as preachers is to declare a divine message that is relevant, significant, and urgent for our times,[15] this weighty responsibility warrants the expansive methods of dissemination God uses to reach humankind. Hebrews 1:1 indicates that God's Word comes to us "in many and various ways" (NRSV). Educators may rightly connect such homiletical theology with the concept of multiple intelligences. Humans hear and process information in multiple ways, through multiple sensory and mental faculties. God, who fashioned us, understands our epistemological diversity. Ancient Hebrew prophets received and proclaimed God's Word in many and various ways, including visions, dreams, parables, pantomimes, and object lessons. The psalmist calls our attention to the eloquence of nature—the heavens, the firmament, the cycles of day and night—all employed as divine messengers proclaiming the glory of God in many and various ways.[16] The Letter to the Hebrews and the Gospel of John both point to that ultimate Word of God who became flesh.[17] This theological gift of incarnation invites us to embody proclamation in forms that are concrete, relatable, and accessible to a diverse spectrum of hearers.

---

15. See Kay, "Theology of Proclamation," in Wilson, *New Interpreter's Handbook of Preaching*, 493–98.

16. Psalm 19:1–3.

17. Hebrews 1:2; John 1:14.

EXPANDING PROCLAMATION

Embodied proclamation is what Lutheran liturgical scholar Carl Schalk reflects upon when he reminds church musicians of Word and Sacrament as ways God speaks through words, water, bread, and wine. He contends that God also speaks through "art, architecture, music, poetry, literature, and various other arts."[18] In clarifying how the reformer Martin Luther viewed music as proclamation, Schalk points out that for Luther praise and proclamation were not just complimentary, they were synonymous. "For Luther praise and proclamation were inextricably linked. To praise God meant to proclaim the good news; conversely to proclaim the good news of the Gospel was precisely the way God was properly praised."[19]

Luther is often quoted as esteeming music as next to theology. Schalk's close reading of this famous maxim is instructive for the claim of this chapter. He interprets this saying of Luther to go beyond a close ranking where theology comes first and is supported by music in a secondary role. "Rather in the combining of the Word with music one is no longer dealing just with music or just with words, but with a third entity in which music and words combine to express in a richer and deeper way what neither words nor music alone can express. The Word brings substance to the music; the music enlivens the Word as 'living voice of the gospel.'"[20] What might it mean to value this third entity as the work of God's hovering Spirit as we put together the elements of our worship services with intention, ensuring that the message of the Word preached and the Word sung are in harmony and not at odds with each other? It might draw our attention to the performative aspect of proclamation.

Homiletician Clayton Schmit helps us conceive of proclamation in its broader sense in his contribution to the edited volume *Performance in Preaching*. Schmit's chapter, "What Comes Next," claims a synonymous relationship between preaching and

---

18. Schalk, "In Many and Various Ways," 12.
19. Schalk, "In Many and Various Ways," 15.
20. Schalk, "In Many and Various Ways," 15.

proclamation. The volume is about preaching, but when it comes to the performative aspect of preaching Schmit explores a definition that fans out beyond pulpit speech. He names several reasons for writing out of this wider scope. The one most critical to our discussion is his third reason: "*Proclamation* suggests, in a way that preaching cannot, that there may be modes of announcing the good news that are not strictly oral discourse."[21] Lest the reader forget the point of this kaleidoscopic examination of proclamation, the breadth of this concept invites us to see that preaching may happen in many and various ways throughout the entire liturgy. If the Word of God comes to us at the will of this speaking God, then proclamation is indeed many-splendored, even artistic.

Lending her voice to this conversation, liturgical scholar Ruth Duck would suggest the collective arts of worship as one effective mode of announcing the good news, more specifically the mystery of the God whom we worship. Duck would argue that if God is as ineffable as we claim God to be, then there are times when art leads us into that ineffable realm better than logic or reasoning. "Through the inspiration of the Spirit and painstaking care, liturgical artists offer worshipers avenues into the sacred through words and beyond words."[22] Congregations benefit from the liturgical art of song and hymn writers every time we gather to worship. These musical sermons proclaim in many and various ways the majesty and mystery of our God. They also proclaim the divine challenge to move from that place of majesty and mystery into a messy world waiting for our worship-inspired action. If pastors and church musicians can embrace this broadened understanding of proclamation, it may infuse more joy into the work of worship planning. And the rippling effect may well result in a congregation of proclaimers. What might a service that proclaims from start to finish look like? Two examples follow, both held at different seminary chapels, each lasting around thirty minutes.

---

21. See Schmit, "What Comes Next," in Childers and Schmit, *Performance in Preaching*, 173.

22. Duck, *Worship for the Whole People*, 83.

Liturgical Integrity

EXAMPLE 1—CHAPEL SERVICE AT PRINCETON THEOLOGICAL SEMINARY

This service was held on November 20, 2012, a day set aside in the liturgical calendar to commemorate the feast of St. Andrew, the apostle. The preacher was James Kay, academic dean of the seminary at that time. Proclamation began from the first note of the organ prelude, John Ferguson's improvisation on "Christ Is the World's Redeemer," a hymn the congregation would sing at the close of the service. Some might wonder how wordless music can proclaim. The notion of musical intelligence supports the idea that persons with musical giftedness can hear God's Word through wordless music.[23] Thomas Troeger believed that the mindful listener could hear God's voice through a musical performance. For Troeger, "a theology that is overly reliant upon words often gives birth to worship that is prosaic and arid. Worship becomes so talky that the expansive mystery and wonder of God have little room to be manifest in the service."[24] Indeed, as the seminary's director of music, Martin Tel, played the organ prelude, it was an invitation into a time of listening for God's voice, whether through silent recall of the hymn text for those who knew it or, for others, through the sonic experience of instrumental praise invoking mystery and wonder.

The call to worship and opening hymn also did proclamatory work. This call to worship included Psalm 19:4, "Their sound has gone out into all lands, and their message to the ends of the world." These sacred words reminded us of the versatility of proclamation. Antecedents of the pronoun "their" in Psalm 19:4 are elements of nature: heavens, firmament, day, and night—they have sound and message. And, like St. Andrew, their message has far-reaching impact.

---

23. No single mode of intelligence functions in isolation, however. Howard Gardner understands that "as an aesthetic form music lends itself especially well to playful exploration with other modes of intelligence and symbolization, particularly in the hands or ears of highly creative individuals" (Gardner, *Frames of Mind*, 126).

24. Troeger, *Wonder Reborn*, 83.

Preaching and Music

This call to worship was followed by Cecil Frances Alexander's hymn "Jesus Calls Us."[25] Alexander's penchant for writing children's hymns that accompany religious education gives her poetry simplicity and directness.[26] Such are the characteristics of the lyrics of "Jesus Calls Us," a hymn she wrote that was inspired by a discussion with her husband around his St. Andrew's Day sermon in 1852.[27] The version of Alexander's hymn in this service included the oft-omitted second verse, "As of old Saint Andrew heard it by the Galilean lake, turned from home and toil and kindred, leaving all for Jesus's sake."[28] In his sermon Kay reiterated and reframed this sense of Andrew's dislocation in response to Christ's call:

> This morning I suspect I am looking out at many dislocated disciples. Many of you have responded to the call of Jesus Christ. In some cases, like Andrew, you have left your occupations, you have left your homelands, whether overseas or in the U.S. And some of you have left the comfort of familiar friends and surroundings, venturing far from the churches or the Christian friends who nurtured you and were always there for you. In the dislocation of God's call, you find yourselves relocated here in different—and sometimes I suspect difficult—terrain.[29]

Such synergy between the sermon and the song made the impact of each that much more effective. The directness of Alexander's poetry, the simple binary format of the hymn tune GALILEE, and the abruptness of Mark's version of this call story all worked in tandem to create an impression strong enough to remain at the forefront of my memory years later.

---

25. Alexander, "Jesus Calls Us," 720.
26. "Cecil Frances Alexander."
27. McAllister, "What Hymn of Discipleship?"
28. Hymnal editors often omit this verse altogether or else replace the reference to St. Andrew with the modification, "As of old apostles heard it." Hawn, "History of Hymns: Jesus Calls Us," para. 19.
29. Kay, "St. Andrew's Day Sermon." Digital file transcribed by author. Subsequent sermonic references all come from this service.

Liturgical Integrity

In this service, sermon and song harmonized to proclaim four sermonic themes: (1) the simplicity and abruptness of Christ's call; (2) the disruption and dislocation that follows; (3) the unpredictability of our relocation, whether geographically or conceptually; and (4) the promise that in following Christ, we are not alone. The Scripture readings were Mark 1:16–17 and John 1:35–42.

In speaking to the abruptness and directness of the call, Kay drew attention to the Markan narrative: "Mark's story is about as abrupt as you can get. It's as abrupt as Christ's call. The story performs for its hearers the very in-breaking of which it tells." A similar literary exegesis may be done on Alexander's hymn. Accustomed as she is to writing for children, her language is uncomplicated and concrete. The first verse states directly, "Jesus calls us; o'er the tumult of our life's wild, restless sea, day by day his clear voice sounding, saying, 'Christian, follow me.'" The other four verses are also simply stated, mirroring Jesus's sparsely worded invitation that belies the complications of following this call.

This led to the preacher's second theme, the disruption and dislocation of the call. Andrew had been a disciple of John up until the call, at which point he made a sharp turn in Jesus's direction. Of this outcome Kay observed, "Christ's call comes as a dislocation; the dislocation of discipleship." Earlier the gathered worshipers sang, "As of old St. Andrew heard it by the Galilean lake, turned from home and toil and kindred, leaving all for Jesus's sake." We had declared this sermonic theme in our congregational singing moments before, the one mode of proclamation reinforcing the other. As Kay preached our subconscious minds would have registered that this is repeated information, thus deepening its impact.

The third move of the sermon emphasized the unpredictability of our relocation, what Kay called our movement into mission. "We do not know in advance of God's calling where it will take us or how God will be present to us in situations we cannot foresee. We do not know ahead of time where discipleship will move us or where it will relocate us on the geographical or the conceptual map." Alexander's message of relocation in her hymn was implicit; one might say it was for those who have ears to hear. She reminded us to hold loosely to life as we know it, trusting that Christ has a better gift for us than the vain world's golden store. She reminded us to prepare ourselves for the unpredictable, looking unto the one who calls us: "In our joys and in our sorrows, days of toil and hours of ease, still he calls in cares and pleasures, 'Christian love me more than these.'"

In the final sermonic move the preacher declared with confidence that we are not alone in following Christ. "Like thousands of others who have been called to Princeton Seminary, and from Princeton Seminary for over 200 years, the God who calls us is faithful and will make a way where there is no way. And we never follow unaccompanied, thanks be to God." The second verse of the final hymn also communicated this point: "Christ has our host surrounded with clouds of martyrs bright, who wave their palms in triumph and fire us for the fight."[30] In keeping with the Scottish ethos of St. Andrew's Day, we tunefully proclaimed words originally penned by St. Columba, a "missionary traditionally credited with the main role in the conversion of Scotland to Christianity."[31] This degree of liturgical integrity was not accidental; the work of the people in this service had been thoughtfully constructed by the worship leaders.

In planning each chapel service, the seminary's minister of the chapel and director of music work with intention toward liturgical integrity. They meet with the preacher weeks ahead for collaborative preparation. As the conversation begins, the preacher sets the tone, indicating what direction they will go with their selected text. Worship planners then comb through their resources, suggesting music and liturgy that generate coherence as the thematic focus begins to sharpen for everyone involved. They check ideas for theological soundness and liturgical efficiency. The outcome is a service of worship where proclamation happens throughout, with thematic integrity.

In reviewing this 2012 St. Andrew's Day service, I could sense the thoughtful, prayerful, collaborative work that had gone into it.

30. Columba, "Christ Is the World's Redeemer," para. 2.
31. Editors of Encyclopedia Britannica, "St. Columba," para. 1.

The words we sang together that day were restatements of good news the preacher wanted us to know and heed long after the service had ended. Cogent thoughts threaded through the sermon were restated explicitly and implicitly throughout the liturgy. The outcome was a fine-tuned example of James Kay's belief, often stated in his seminary classes, that the proclamation of the gospel in worship is far too important a task to be undertaken exclusively by the sermon.

EXAMPLE 2—CHAPEL SERVICE AT LANCASTER THEOLOGICAL SEMINARY

This 2023 chapel service, designed by students at the seminary, was developed around the theme of "Salt and Light," taken from Matthew 5:13–16. The service culminated a day and a half of intensive orientation for new students. The theme focused on the unique identity of each student, affirming the particular flavor and luminescence each one would introduce to our seminary community. This was their introduction to the chapel space and the tenor of community worship, which they could hope to experience every Saturday morning just before going to class. Considering their fatigue after being overwhelmed by densely packaged information, the liturgy was designed to last around thirty minutes. The sermon was titled "Let Me Tell You Why You're Here," a quote from the opening line of Eugene Peterson's paraphrase of the Matthew scripture.

The opening song was an invocation, not directly sharing the proclamation of the theme but issuing an important declaration nonetheless. Its primary function was to center and ground the students after exhausting sessions packed with information, some of which was bound to introduce doubts about their readiness for seminary. The gentle Taizé chant was both invocation and declaration: "Come and fill our hearts with your peace. You alone, O Lord, are holy. Come and fill our hearts with your peace, alleluia!"[32]

---

32. Taizé Community, "Come and Fill Our Hearts," hymn 466.

Preaching and Music

Accompanied by an acoustic guitar, this chant did what opening music can do best—it created a welcoming moment, the invitation to divest the mind of all that troubles and distracts. The chant proclaimed that God alone is holy, and that this holy God was there to fill the worshipers' hearts with divine peace.

The welcome and opening prayer that followed were extemporaneously done by the director of chapel worship, who welcomed the students into this spiritual space. The Call to Worship was a call and response declaration of our Christian identity as salt and light. The students' liturgical responses echoed the Matthew passage, "We are the salt of the earth. We are the light of the world" (Matthew 5:13–14).

Bernadette Farrell's "Christ Be Our Light" was the opening hymn. Farrell's passion for social justice drives the proclamation in this hymn, with its petition for Christ's light to shine through us. As the students launched into the final verse, they prayerfully declared, "Many the gifts, many the people, many the hearts that yearn to belong. Let us be servants to one another, making your kingdom come."[33] Minutes later they would hear this thought rephrased and reiterated as I declared in my sermon's close,

> Your flavor and brilliance matter when we consider ways to do prison ministry and chaplaincy in hospitals to all different kinds of people. Your flavor and brilliance matter when we discuss theology because theology is the way we understand God. And if God is as incomprehensible and ineffable as we say God is, then far from being a fixed set of beliefs, theology is more like an ongoing conversation, to which you now add your own perspective. Your God-flavor and your unique reflection of God's brilliance matter here—we are all dim-sighted believers, touching a different part of the proverbial elephant, as we together figure it out.[34]

The prayer of confession, a poetic reading, and the reading of the Scripture all harmonized around Jesus's call to be our authentic

---

33. Farrell, "Christ Be Our Light," 114.
34. Williams, "Let Me Tell You Why You're Here."

Liturgical Integrity

selves—our brand of salt and our kind of light—as we show up in the world. The final song, "This Little Light of Mine,"[35] reiterated the call of the opening hymn and the thrust of the sermon. Brief though this service was, its effectiveness and impact were created by its coherence around a consistent message. Students reported being affirmed by the experience. It settled them and quieted the voice of the imposter syndrome in their heads. The service had barely ended before parts of it were posted by students on social media.

Whether planned months in advance, or mapped mentally the week before, our services are more meaningful and memorable when coherent. The opposite of such intentionality would be randomness, where songs, prayers, and other elements of the service are discrete, having no bearing on one another; heaven forbid, they may even contradict one another! We want to avoid the impression that the service is a collection of empty rituals done without thought of anything else happening around them, and that the only thing of real importance is the sermon. Coherence ties the liturgical elements together with integrity so that they perform in harmony; they complement one another so that the impact of the whole is more wonderful than the sum of its parts. Randomness often happens when different ones responsible for parts of the service make choices without checking in with what others are doing. Coherence, on the other hand, often happens when service planners or worship leaders work as a team, with the goal of liturgical integrity.

PLANNING FOR LITURGICAL INTEGRITY

Team-based worship design is essential to effective liturgy, which, by definition, is the work of the people—implying at least more than one person involved. Collaboration ideally provides checks and balances against the kind of weekly outcome where one person's tastes and ideas prevail every Sunday. Different vantage points need to come together for this variation on the theme of preaching and music to have impact. When pastors or church

---

35. African American spiritual, public domain.

musicians think of service planning or worship design, personal preferences may influence how they approach this process. The organizer who enjoys planning will take to this naturally, while the more spontaneous leader might resist this notion of working on a service days or weeks ahead.

Admittedly, in some cases collaboration is difficult, particularly these days when pandemic-induced changes have laid heavy administrative burdens upon solo pastors and part-time church staff. Yet any effort at collaborative planning, no matter how small, yields worthwhile dividends. It covers blind spots, gives unfamiliar perspectives a chance to refresh our understanding of God, and approaches the liturgy from different directions so planners can see it from multiple vantage points. Take, for example, the vantage point of disabled or differently abled persons. There are some prayers, scripture passages, readings, and hymn lyrics that may sound appropriate to persons whose physical or mental abilities are socially normalized. The same words may register harshly or inappropriately with disabled persons, rendering disability as a problem to be solved, or, worse yet, co-relating it with sin or evil. Someone on a worship planning team attuned to the sensibilities of disabled persons will catch the faulty word or phrase in the planning or review process, suggesting a more hospitable alternative. Team-based worship design is worth the effort if worship is to be meaningful to all God's people.

Collaboration also brings different musical memory banks to the table. This increases the likelihood of selecting the most fitting song or musical piece; it lightens the burden of the pastor or musician. As the preacher shares ideas about where the sermon is heading, a word or phrase might evoke another person's memory of a hymn or song whose lines may be used anywhere in the service: call to worship, liturgical response or affirmation, benediction, or as a musical component. In a collaborative planning process the pastor or church musician does not need to have all the answers; indeed, this can be liberating.

If not used to the framework of liturgical integrity or coherence, a solo pastor might be intimidated by the amount of time it

Liturgical Integrity

takes to look for or compose prayers and songs that point in the same direction as the scripture or the theme. Strategies that might make this process easier for a solo pastor include (1) available practical resources, (2) identifying one or two collaborators, and (3) a planning template for moving from start to finish.

Available Practical Resources

If a church uses a hymnal, or at least if hymns are part of the congregational repertoire, the hymnal indexes are a handy resource. Located at the back of most hymnals, indexes are a quick way to find congregational music by topic, author, scripture, tune, meter, liturgical season, lectionary readings, and other useful categories. If some of these categories are not available in the church's hymnal, the pastor may purchase a couple of other hymnals with multiple, helpful indexes for the sake of access to appropriate music. And if the hymns found have great lyrics but they are unknown to the congregation, that pastor has choices. She may either choose to teach it to the congregation, or, using the metrical index, pair the lyrics with a familiar tune, or she may just use some of the lyrics in her sermon, the call to worship, or a prayer. Use of the hymnal's metrical index is explained more fully in chapter 2.

Online databases are another resource for finding music that keeps the service coherent. The free website hymnary.org is one such resource. For contemporary Christian music, or music in the praise and worship genre, the church could benefit from a subscription to a copyright licensing agency such as CCLI or OneLicense. Such resources have extensive searchable databases containing a variety of congregational music, along with other helpful, related features. Pastors who care about liturgical integrity may encounter certain limitations as they browse through digital resources in the contemporary Christian music genre. One issue tends to be the narrow thematic or theological focus in this category of church music. As a genre, praise and worship music does not cover well the wide range of topics available in a hymnal index. The pastor browsing through contemporary Christian music for songs that proclaim jointly with the sermon may have to look beyond the titles to find an idea that may be buried in the lyrics. As an example, the title of Matt Redman's hit song, "10,000 Reasons" does not give away much. Yet there are allusions to verses of Psalm 103 that make this song a liturgical gem, including its poignant end-of-life reflections buried in the song's third verse: "And on that day when my strength is failing, the end is near and my time has come, still my soul will sing your praise unending, ten thousand years and then forevermore."[36]

Volunteer Collaborators

A solo pastor of a small congregation might be wondering, "How can I do this without a staff?" Kathy, who is now paid as a church musician, did this work as a volunteer in a former congregation.[37] She and the pastor would have email or text conversations about the service. Based on his theme or scripture focus, she would reply with song suggestions. As a reminder, this approach works for the pastor who is at least a week ahead of the worship service. If solo pastor John wants to try this more liturgically integrated approach and is used to settling on his theme or scripture three days before the service, he might make himself accountable to that volunteer who will check in on him ten to fourteen days ahead. Using the lectionary readings or seasons of the liturgical calendar is a great way to achieve this coherence. The Revised Common Lectionary facilitates advance planning, since part of the liturgical work is already in place thanks to many denominational websites and printed planning resources. Think of these online resources as collaborators! They come to the planning process with preconceived ideas, which the pastor or musician is free to accept, reject, or tweak, based on the specific makeup of the congregation and the direction in which the Sunday service is headed.

---

36. Redman and Myrin, "10,000 Reasons."
37. Kathy Collier, in conversation with author, February 28, 2022.

Liturgical Integrity

Some solo pastors have met this need for teamwork by coming together with other pastors of small congregations, sharing their resources and ideas. Some of these ministerium groups happen face to face early in the week, while others happen through social media like Facebook or Instagram. In my preaching classes, students who are used to working on their own are often surprised and energized by the exponential learning and ease of thought that happens when a group of them collaborate to exegete a scripture passage or plan a service. Many of them who are pastors resolve to find or start a similar group for their weekly work. One or two other preachers or musicians is all it takes.

I encourage solo pastors who have no paid music staff to prayerfully seek one or two people who can cast another pair of eyes over the service to add musical perspective. They may be working or retired music teachers or music aficionados in the congregation who have a large mental database of songs and who love talking about music. They may be English teachers, poets, or deep readers of prose and poetry. They may be teenagers who are really into music and can add a missing youthful component to the service. Conversations with these helpers may revolve around two questions: What songs would help proclaim the message of this scripture passage or this theme? How best can this song be rendered in this service—solo, instrumental, solo and congregation, or ensemble or choir? I encourage pastors of hymn-loving congregations to be open to music outside the hymnal. People's lives are surrounded, some even saturated, by music. We are influenced by music from movies, TV shows, musicals, plays, and myriad other sources. Any music that helps us make connections between the liturgy and people's lives deserves consideration.

Using a Template

For the busy pastor or worship planning team, use of a weekly template can significantly reduce planning time. Like any set pattern a template can always be adapted for special occasions or seasonal services. However, being able to plug in music, prayers, and other parts of the service in a preset structure can offer a sense of consistency. Two or three different templates may be used to avoid the infamous rut.[38] Some churches go the digital route and purchase subscriptions to online planning resources. Some of these have search features and are able to generate reports from archived services, revealing, for example, how often the congregation has sung certain hymns in a given time period. A template can be a time-saving device; it can also be a visual aid toward liturgical integrity.

PASTOR-MUSICIAN TALKING POINTS

These reflections offer prompts for conversations around lyrical theology, the language of hymns, and decision making around sung or spoken proclamation, all toward enhanced liturgical integrity.

Lyrical Theology

In the preacher-musician partnership theology is generally the area of study the preacher has engaged while songs lie more squarely within the musician's study and/or experience. These two areas of spiritual focus come together in lyrical theology, a term that eloquently names the partnered work of preacher and musician. Methodist scholar S. T. Kimbrough uses this term to frame the concept of hymns of the church as theological statements. They are, he argues, "the church's lyrical, theological commentaries on scripture liturgy, faith, action, and hosts of other subjects which call the reader and singer to faith, life, and Christian practice."[39] Tom Troeger, preacher and hymn composer, would agree. In arguing for hymns as *midrashim* that do a particular kind of interpretive work, Troeger writes from his personal perspective as

---

38. Among many accessible suggestions for the way worship may be ordered, see Costen's Worship Model, in *African American Christian Worship*, 122–25; Liu and Williams's Model for Planning Together, in *Worship Workbook*, 132–34; Miller's basic order for Sunday worship in *New Pastor's Guide*, 31; and Duck, *Worship for the Whole People of God*, 66.

39. Kimbrough, "Hymns Are Theology," 59.

Liturgical Integrity

a preacher, pastor, and poet: "Hymns usually grow out of efforts to interpret scripture and theology in poetically beautiful, easily accessible, and pastorally empowering ways."[40] Many reading this book would agree that much of what we understand and believe about God—for good or for ill—has been distilled through the songs we sing in worship. Whether intentionally or unwittingly, whether explicitly or implicitly, all our congregational songs proclaim or teach something about God or God's activity in the world. Hence the importance of the collaborative work of the pastor and musician. This knowing God through music is at least as ancient as the psalms.

Lyrical theology is what the psalms expressed for temple worshipers in the ancient world and for first-century Christians who brought their old songs into their new faith. These songs captured a range of human conditions in prayers, praises, celebrations, and laments that endeared them to the worshipers. They gave meaning to individual and national conundrums. They were to the Jewish worshipers what the spirituals were to enslaved Africans in the United States. They embraced both lament and hope, dreams and despair, tragedy and triumph. Their poetry made them memorable and quotable. How meaningful that in the throes of death Jesus borrowed language from two of these songs of his faith to express himself. His cry, "My God, my God, why have you forsaken me," is the opening line of Psalm 22, and his final gasp of "Father, into your hands I commit my spirit" comes from Psalm 31:5. Psalms feature in almost every genre of New Testament writings, either as direct quotes or allusions—because sometimes, when we need to plumb theological depths or soar to theological heights, only a song will do!

There is the theological work done through study and discussion facilitated by classrooms and colleagues. Then there is the theological work done in the midst of life as we call upon embedded understandings to give meaning to our often-perplexing situations. It is in these moments that try our faith that the faith we sing does its theological work. Pastor and musicians are a strong team

40. Troeger, *Wonder Reborn*, 30.

when they together understand that because psalms, hymns, and spiritual songs do theology in such succinct, accessible ways, they make great partners in proclamation.

Use of Language

Both preaching and music use words to communicate. While the preacher is free to choose language in a sermon that is sensitive to the congregation's needs, the musician needs to scrutinize the congregation's songs for language and imagery that may unintentionally cause harm or reflect neglect. Such is the case with biblical references to blind and lame people that suggest these disabilities are sinful. Pastors and musicians do care-filled work when they examine the words to be sung considering who will be listening, whether in the pews or online. One musician spoke of being aware that there are some well-loved hymns whose language is misaligned with the congregation's values. She tries to have a balance. "I will go to bat for old, beloved hymns that are in our congregation's DNA and we don't have another way of singing them, yet I think they are important to sing. I consider the entire worship service when that happens, ensuring that other parts of the service offset the dated nature of that particular hymn."[41] This is a critical occasion for collaborative assessment. The pastor may decide to go ahead with the problematic but beloved hymn, using it as an opportunity for a teaching moment in worship. If used as is, a note in the bulletin or a verbal introduction can indicate the troubling language and state what might be a more appropriate wording. Or the verse may be omitted altogether. Prayerful, thoughtful collaboration around this issue aims for theological consistency and liturgical integrity in the proclaimed Word, spoken and sung.

---

41. Kathy Collier, conversation with the author, February 28, 2022.

Liturgical Integrity

Voicing Scriptures and Liturgy

Pastor-musician conversations may also touch on how the liturgy will be voiced. Understanding how music can enrich proclamation and how congregational participation can enliven meaning, the pastor and musician team may comb through a scripted service for ways to achieve liturgical integrity. If there is an anthem or congregational song whose lyrics render the scripture verbatim, the worship planners may negotiate how much of the scripture is read and how much is sung. For example, Mary's song in Luke 1:46–55 has generated so many hymns, choral pieces, or solos, it is possible that the reading of Scripture may be shared between a reader and singer, or reader and choir, or reader and congregational hymn such as Cooney's "My Soul Cries Out with a Joyful Shout."[42] With care-filled collaboration that values the proclamatory function of music throughout the service, the scripture text may come to life and land in a different way when sung. The same principle holds for other parts of the liturgy. The call to worship may be the words of a psalm or hymn, spoken or sung. The prayers of the people may be in a call and response pattern where the people's response is a refrain such as, "Lord, listen to your children praying."[43] Occasionally even the benediction may be rendered musically by the congregation. These conversations around supplementing speech with song underscore the value of proclamation in many and various ways.

CONCLUSION

This chapter has focused on the benefits of liturgical integrity, recommending that sermon and song synergize thematically or scripturally. The question may well arise, does every song have to proclaim the same message? Or put another way, where is there room for a song selection that simply embodies our faith and supports our daily Christian life because of memories, values, and

---

42. Cooney, "Canticle of the Turning," 18.
43. Medema, "Lord Listen to Your Children Praying," 469.

Preaching and Music

beliefs attached to its text and tune?[44] Duck is referring to what some call heart songs, beloved texts and tunes that have deep congregational history, songs folks know by heart. This chapter would not be complete without brief reflection on these questions. If every service were so tightly designed with music that proclaims only what the sermon is about, or music tightly connected with the day's theme or season, many beloved, meaningful songs would hardly be used in worship. The wisdom around this suggests that there are times a worship service should have some musical space for songs that offer care for the soul, reinforce creedal beliefs, or simply praise God for no reason other than that God is always worthy of all praise. Fastidious attention to sermonic seamlessness in a service can feel inorganic, with no room for the breath of the Spirit to blow through the liturgy. Sometimes a preacher may insert a pre-sermonic hymn that is simply invocational, its sole function being to capture a sense of divine energy that will help launch the preaching moment. Purposeful worship planning is also prayerful planning, which makes collaboration vital.

The weight or import of proclamation is too great to be borne by the sermon exclusively. "The whole worship service, rather than just the sermon, is a proclamation of the Word."[45] This informs our purposeful selection and placement of musical proclamation. It also requires the kind of thought and care facilitated by a collaborative approach to preparing the order of worship. Such care will inevitably call for an expansion of congregational repertoire, a subject dealt with in the following chapter on framing the sermon.

---

44. Duck, *Worship for the Whole People*, 87.

45. See Meyers, "Worship Amplifies the Voice of the Preacher," in Greenhaw and Allen, *Preaching in the Context of Worship*, 9.

2

Framing the Sermon

MANY OF US AS preachers have experienced the vibrant synergy that happens when the music in closest proximity to the sermon aligns with the sermon's focus and its function. In support of this idea I use the metaphor of framing for some insight into the selection of music immediately surrounding the sermon. In this chapter we look closely at focus and function as touch points in sermon design that keep the preacher on track and guide musical selection. We discuss how to make suitable musical choices and what to do when a limited congregational playlist makes such choices difficult. The chapter ends with discussion points that this framing work generates between pastor and musician, giving helpful ways to introduce new music into the congregation's canon.

This homiletical theory of focus and function, taken from Tom Long's writing and explained later in the chapter,[1] can expand the sermonic delivery to include a hymn of preparation and a hymn of response. When selected well, this music anticipates the sermon's main idea, increases its impact, and provides a way for

1. Long, *Witness of Preaching*, 114–15.

the listener to continue hearing the sermon long after the preacher has spoken the last word. This blend of preaching and music has been known to turn the sermon's main idea into a musical earworm; it has also been known to finish an incomplete sermon.

One of my colleagues provided me with an example of this kind of synergy. He recalled preaching a sermon that was nowhere near the rhetorical craft of his usual delivery. It had been a difficult week in a stressful season. Day after day, unplanned events eroded his usual preparation time until he found himself at the Sunday pulpit disappointed in the sermon before he had even spoken the first word. He faithfully walked the dog anyway. After he sat down, the person who had been leading the singing followed her impulse to lead the congregation in an unplanned selection inspired by the preaching. My colleague recalls the significant shift of energy in the room once voices, lifted in song, began to complete the sermonic message. In a moment of incomplete ending, that impromptu song did everything the sermon needed to do in its closing moments; it rounded out the proclamation.

This chapter argues for such a dynamic partnership between sermon and song, using the metaphor of framing. Songs that appropriately frame the sermon can be an extension of the preacher's voice. Sermon and song, homily and hymn—they assist each other to proclaim the good news of the gospel, doing together what neither of them can do alone.

FRAMES

The concept of framing is understood by certified professional framers, persons who have gone through a certification process giving them the skills for framing artwork, enclosing it in a mount that enhances its beauty and value. People who prepare works of art for display understand that among the many external factors that affect how the art is viewed, the frame is most critical. One journal advises that "the frame of a picture should be so made that its colour [sic] and texture should support and reinforce the effect of the work of the artist, by rendering the force and tenderness of tint and form more expressive."[2] Frames, whether inexpensively store-bought or expensively custom-made, do particular work around a photo or a visual artist's creation. Granted, the metaphor may not be entirely transferable to sermon framing since picture framers assume a clear hierarchy between the picture and its frame, the latter being subordinate artistically to the former. Yet there is a sense, without being hierarchical, that the content of the sermon is what determines the music that will frame it, even if some listeners get the message more effectively through one over the other.

Art frames are meant to bring out the best of what they enclose, to invite the beholder to pay attention in specific ways. A rustic frame of natural wood may call attention to the rural beauty of a log cabin next to an old, stately oak tree. An ornate beveled black and gold frame may amplify the majestic poise and rich attire of an Elizabethan woman of means, picking up the hues of her clothing, magnifying the impression of nobility. It has been said that "well-considered framing may enhance the appearance of even an indifferent work of art."[3] Thus, a crudely taken snapshot of a mother hugging a child with a cluttered kitchen in the background can become a poignant memory within a frame engraved with the words "Family is where love begins." Studying these different frames, we can imagine why the family frame will not work with the log cabin painting, or the ornate beveled frame with the mother and child in the kitchen. This concept of framing clarifies the efficacy of music placed before and after the sermon. It can enrich, or it can erode. It can support, or it can sabotage. Thoughtful worship planning determines which.

Thoughtful worship planning is mindful of the needs of the flock who will gather to be tended in worship. Many who gather resonate with the filling-station metaphor for corporate worship. The week has emptied their spiritual and emotional fuel supply; they come on Sunday needing to be restored, refreshed, and revived. For some, the week may have challenged what they thought they believed about God, and they come on Sunday needing to

2. "On the Framing of Pictures," 162–63.
3. A. T., "Framing of Pictures," 90.

hear once more the good news of the gospel, that God is, and is for them. For still others, they may be numbed into complacency by yet another tragedy in their lives, their community, the nation, or the world. Their need on Sunday morning is to be reinvigorated, to be strengthened anew for their mission of showing Christ's love in the world. Thoughtful worship planners do their best to tune into the congregational ethos, to determine what people need to say to God and what God might say to God's people in these times and on this occasion. Therefore, intentionality around liturgical and musical selections needs to be part of the preacher's sermon preparation process. As it did for my colleague, and as it does for so many preachers every Sunday, the music may serve as the capstone of the sermonic moment, where the sermon becomes embodied and embedded in the hearers. Some may see the music in this way as an appendage to the sermon, but there is homiletical theory that supports this flow and connection.

HOMILETICAL THEORY

Tom Long, in his seminal preaching volume, devotes an entire chapter to the concepts of focus and function. Long believes the sermon has something to say and do, based on the claim of the selected text upon the hearers. This claim is not some static idea, the same voice or message we hear every time we read that text. Rather it is that compelling, occasion-specific concept that arises from careful exegesis: "It is what we hear on *this day*, from *this text*, for *these people*, in *these circumstances*, at *this juncture in their lives*."[4] In moving from establishing the claim to crafting the sermon, Long suggests developing focus and function statements—the focus identifying what the sermon hopes to say and the function naming what the sermon hopes to do.

---

4. Long, *Witness of Preaching*, 114–15.

Framing the Sermon

Focus

Compelling preaching leaves an impression on the hearer. Five minutes, five hours, five days, weeks, or even months after such a sermon, the hearer can recall and repeat the gist of what they heard. I acknowledge that what the preacher means for people to hear and what they *do* hear is often different; end-of-service exchanges with congregants provide ample evidence of this phenomenon. However, it is possible to have such a clear focus to the sermon that anyone paying attention, from youngest to oldest, gets the point. Establishing the sermon's focus is important because of what we are doing in preaching. We are proclaiming the good news of God. We are interpreting the Word of God, giving the sense of it (Nehemiah 8:8) to the people. Given such a task, it is the preacher's responsibility to get at the heart of that word for that occasion. The late Dr. Samuel Proctor puts it this way, "Before any sermon goes anywhere, the preacher must have focus and direction. Although the idea should be potent enough to be broken down into subtopics, a tangible, simple statement must be written down saying that *this is what I shall have said when I am finished.*"[5] Seasoned as well as novice preachers know how easy it can be for a sermon to go everywhere at once. As we open commentaries and click on links to online resources, we can end up with a great deal of fascinating material that can make us sound well-informed. Yet the truth is we would have spent more time assimilating that information than our listeners who will hear it only once. Multiple important concepts interwoven into an informative, well-resourced delivery can make a sermon sound more like a lecture or speech. A sermon becomes more memorable when it presents one focused, well-supported thought.

"Focus, Jonathan!" is the directive often given to my grandson who has the remarkable capacity to seemingly notice everything all at once. His attention becomes diffuse. It is like pulling teeth to get his response to the question of the moment, "Where are your shoes?" By asking him to focus, his mother is attempting

---

5. Proctor, *Certain Sound*, 26.

to direct his attention to the thing that matters most then and there if they are to make it to church on time. "Focus, Jonathan" is like asking him to use a telescope rather than a kaleidoscope. Many of us in the pews are there with kaleidoscopic attention; between life's demands and the liturgy's demands on our senses, it is easy to tune out during an unfocused monologue that lasts anywhere from ten to thirty minutes. The preacher who has taken the time to determine "what it is I shall have said when I am finished" has an easier time engaging and keeping our attention. How might the preacher establish such clarity?

Let us use a well-known parable as an example. Luke 15:11–32 tells the story of the Lost Son, often called the Prodigal Son. We hear of a man who has two sons, the younger of whom cashes in on his rightful inheritance and uses it all up in a place far from home. At some point this son comes to himself, returns home, and is given a lavish welcome by his father. The second son stumbles upon the celebration of his younger brother's return and becomes angry. The parable ends with the father trying to persuade the older sibling of his love for both sons, urging him to see things in a different light. How many sermons or Bible lessons have we heard on this parable? How many have we preached or taught ourselves? If we grew up in Sunday school or church, we have probably lost count. However, I remember very specifically the one sermon on this story that was life-changing—almost thirty years ago now. I remember the preacher's focus because that is what caught hold of my heart. The sermon shined its spotlight on the attitude of the father toward his sons. I imagine if my pastor had written his focus statement on an index card and kept it before him while he outlined his sermon, it may have read something like "Notice the welcoming attitude of the father toward a son who did not deserve it." That point registered with me, especially the "did not deserve it" part, because of a relational struggle I was trying to resolve as I sat listening that day. The preacher's point was strong and repeatable.

A focus statement should be concise enough that someone can say it in one sentence or two to the person who missed church and asked what the sermon was about. It should capture the one thing the preacher wants the hearer to understand if nothing else. Another focus statement on the same parable might be about the idea of being lost and then found; it can state: "We are to hold on to hope when all seems lost." Another, emphasizing the possibility that both sons were lost, might read: "We can be lost, far from the father's home, or lost, far from the father's heart." If the preacher's use of the Revised Common Lectionary has taken them to this text one time too often, they may find it useful to read this story in places not typical for them. It could be in a kitchen, a garage, a garden, a coffee shop, a church parking lot, or the waiting room of a doctor's office. Often a shift in physical location casts a different light on a well-known text, causing words, images, or ideas to pop with fresh meaning, providing a different focus.[6] It is often in those moments of *lectio divina* that an idea begins to grip the preacher's heart or mind. That may well be the claim of the text for this occasion and for these people. What would you hope to say about that claim that listeners can put into action? Capture that idea in one, no more than two sentences; that becomes the sermon's focus statement—at least for now. Focus statements are prone to being tweaked as the sermon develops.

It is a good idea, for novice and seasoned preachers alike, to have this statement written down, either at the top of an electronic document, or on an index card or sticky note kept in view as the sermon takes shape. Having a central, guiding idea around a text or theme gives the sermon a sense of direction. I have experienced writing a sermon whose focus I thought was fully formed in my mind, only to get one third or halfway through to find my thoughts beginning to sound scattered, going in several directions at once—a sure sign of lack of focus. However, if before beginning to write I have put that central idea into a statement, I can either tweak that statement to reflect the most compelling of my emerging ideas or I can return to the point in my writing where I was still on track. At that moment I may cut the rest of the writing and set it aside to either redirect it toward my compelling idea or save it for

---

6. Troeger and Tisdale, *Sermon Workbook*, 141.

Preaching and Music

another sermon. My sermon writing goes best when I know where the sermon is going.

In refining a statement of focus it helps to ask:

- Is it clear?
- Is it concise—contained in one or two simple sentences?
- Is it something a listener can repeat five days or weeks later?
- Are there key words that make it cogent or compelling?

The Music

If by now in the writing process a song has not already begun providing some background music, the next step would be to find a song that captures or reinforces the sermon's focus. This would be sung before the preaching; its role is to orient the listeners in the sermon's direction. Let's return to the example of the preacher who asked me to pay attention to the attitude of the father toward a son who did not deserve it. What words might describe such an attitude? Mercy? Forgiveness? Grace? Acceptance? Welcome? If we use those as search words in a topical index of a hymnal, or in a digital database of congregational songs, here are some songs we might find: "Amazing Grace," or "There's a Wideness in God's Mercy," or "Your Grace Is Enough."

In the process of making the right selection we need a critical eye. Sometimes a song title hints at one idea, but the lyrics take us in another direction. The welcoming attitude of the father requires a song that focuses on the father more so than the son. If so, then Newton's "Amazing Grace," as poignant as it is, would not be as strong a choice as Matt Maher's "Your Grace Is Enough." Newton's lyrics cast the spotlight on the grace-receiver: "Amazing grace, how sweet the sound that saved a wretch like *me*. *I* once was lost, but now am found, was blind but now *I* see."[7] In Maher's lyrics, however, the spotlight is on the grace-giver: "Great is *your* faithfulness

---

7. Newton, "Amazing Grace," 378.

oh *God, you* wrestle with the sinner's restless heart. *You* lead us by still waters into mercy, and nothing can keep us apart."[8] If the focus of the sermon is on the grace-giver, then the more fitting song of preparation will point in that direction.

This music, sung before the sermon, serves as a sort of weather vane or windsock—both show which way the wind is blowing. The song points to the sermon's focus and helps orient the listener—mentally and spiritually—in that direction. The synergy between song and sermon amplifies the total impact. Such anticipatory music may happen anywhere from the beginning of the service to the preaching moment. But it is most effective just before the reading of Scripture or before the sermon. In the liturgy it may be called the hymn of preparation, hymn of reflection, or sermonic selection. In some churches this music has an invocational role; the preacher draws on the spiritual energy of this song to launch into preaching. This sung invocation can be conceived as a musical prayer of illumination, casting a spotlight on the claim of the Scripture that has informed the homily's focus. A musical start makes for a compelling sermon.

Function

If the focus of the sermon is, simply put, the *what* of the sermon—what the preacher hopes to say—then the function points to the *why* of the sermon—what the preacher hopes the sermon will do in and through those who hear it. Surely the Holy Spirit at work as the Word is proclaimed can cause a sermon to function in as many ways as there are people listening to it. Even so, the faithful preacher who has taken time to identify the focus of the sermon will take the next step to imagine what kind of response might be fitting. The faithful preacher asks herself or himself, *What would it look like if people really heard this sermon well enough to put it into action?* According to Long,

---

8. Maher, "Your Grace Is Enough," 698.

Preaching and Music

A function statement is a description of what the preacher hopes the sermon will create or cause to happen for the hearers. Sermons make demands upon the hearers, which is another way of saying that they provoke change in the hearers (even if the change is a deepening of something already present). The function statement names the hoped-for change.[9]

The answer to the question of why something exists is a clue to its function. I like to drink my tea in a double-walled teacup. It was designed with a double wall so hot drinks would keep their temperature longer. That would be the function or why of my double-walled teacup. Homiletically, function considers the why. *Why go through the trouble of preparing and preaching this sermon*, the preacher would do well to ask. *What is the reason for preaching this sermon*, is another way to phrase the question. *What do I hope this sermon will do?*

The strongest answers begin with a verb: to encourage, to warn, to challenge, to invite, to comfort, to persuade, to open a new perspective on, to help people see, think, act, trust, and so on. A purposeful function tends to guide how the sermon ends. You might say the function orients the listener toward a response of some kind, whether it be reflection, action, or change. Hearing what the sermon says with no suggestion of what to do about it can leave listeners in the category of the self-deceiving persons the Apostle James writes about, who observe what they look like in a mirror and walk away, forgetting what they saw that needs attention.[10] Compelling preaching moves us to respond. John the Baptist's preaching drove his listeners to ask, "What then should we do?" (Luke 3:10). Peter's moving Pentecost sermon provoked the same response; "Brothers, what should we do?" (Acts 2:37). To have our listeners be hearers and doers of the Word we sharpen the impact of what they hear with the sermon's focus and help them respond or do something about it with the sermon's function.

---

9. Long, *Witness of Preaching*, 109.
10. James 1:23–24.

Framing the Sermon

Liturgist Constance Cherry offers a theology of response in her book *The Worship Architect*. Cherry sees the "engagement of revelation and response [as forming] the core of Christian worship."[11] She invites worship planners to conceive of worship as a dialogical encounter between God and the gathered—a call-and-response encounter, if you will. God calls and invites us to worship, and we respond. Our responses include prayers, litanies, songs, and actions such as giving our bodies in movement or our monetary gifts in the offering. While Cherry advocates our approach to the Communion Table as the primary response to hearing the Word, she allows that in some congregations where weekly communion is not part of the service there are other fitting responses to the Word. The purpose of this moment in worship, she says, "is to communicate our response to God as a result of having heard and received God's word in worship."[12]

The hymn following the sermon, when well chosen, can support the people's response to hearing God's word; it provides the language and attitude of response fitting for the moment. Thus, if the focus of my prodigal son sermon is the attitude of the father, the function might be to inspire or encourage my listeners toward a disposition of mercy—treating others better than they deserve.

If I hope my sermon would function to inspire a merciful attitude, then a fitting hymn of reflection might be Fred Kaan's "Help Us Accept Each Other." The first verse says, "Help us accept each other as Christ accepted us; teach us as sister, brother, each person to embrace. Be present, Lord, among us, and bring us to believe we are ourselves accepted and meant to love and live."[13] In this prayerful response the congregation acknowledges that adopting a disposition of mercy is difficult; they are requesting divine help to accept others as they themselves have been accepted.

Another hymn choice might be the second verse of John Peacey's hymn "Go Forth for God," which says, "Go forth for God, go to the world in love; strengthen the faint, give courage to the

---

11. Cherry, *Worship Architect*, 19.
12. Cherry, *Worship Architect*, 117.
13. Kaan, "Help Us Accept Each Other," 560.

weak; help the afflicted; richly from above God's love supplies the grace and power we seek. Go forth for God, go to the world in love."[14] These words call the singers to action. They echo the divine mandate of showing love to our neighbors; they also give assurance of divine grace as we do the often-difficult work of love.

A topical index at the back of a hymnal or the key word "mercy" in a digital search field are both good starting places for selecting a song that echoes the sermon's function. This call to action may also be reflected in the closing or sending song that rounds out the worship service. One qualifying characteristic of response music is familiarity—how well the singers know the song. Because this is often a moment of heart engagement with the preached word, the song that facilitates the response to the Word is most effective when it is familiar, when the congregation can sing it from the heart. Knowing this invites the preacher to know something of the congregation's musical canon or playlist.

Pastor and theological educator Rochelle Stackhouse encourages preachers to become familiar with their congregational playlist of known songs. Stackhouse believes,

> Just as the preacher works to build familiarity with the Bible, so too . . . the preacher would benefit by building a strong repertoire of hymn texts from which to draw inspiration, theological material, playful language, and most especially, a way into the ears and minds of congregants who may be much more familiar with hymns than with the Bible.[15]

I would press her choice of musical repertoire beyond the category of hymns. The popular music genre generously provides themes and points of reflection that connect with our listeners.

One preacher ended her sermon on love with "Seasons of Love" from the musical *Rent*: "Five hundred twenty-five thousand six hundred minutes, five hundred twenty-five thousand moments so dear." The function was contained in the song's final question:

14. Peacey, "Go Forth for God," 670.
15. See Stackhouse, "Music, Proclamation, and Praise," in Greenhaw and Allen, *Preaching in the Context of Worship*, 97.

"In five hundred twenty-five thousand six hundred minutes, how do you measure a year in a life? How about love? How about love? How about love? Measure in love . . . seasons of love."[16] People still come up to her years later and quote from that sermon that reminded them of their identity marker as God's children—people who love God and neighbor.

Another preacher ended his sermon to new seminary students with Bill Withers's "Use Me Up," expressing the kind of irrational attachment we have to the often-unrewarding work God calls us to do as pastors and spiritual leaders. The function of that sermon was to affirm and encourage vocational abandon. While neither congregation sang these two examples, the musical-homiletical value was real. One student on her way out of worship was heard to say, "I love me some Bill Withers, I'll be singing that song now." In so many words she was saying, "This sermon will keep on preaching now." Whether quoted at the sermon's close or sung afterward, if the music happens to be an earworm or has a hook that captures the sermon's call to action, it adds enduring value to the sermon, making it memorable.

Embodied Musical Response

In some churches an altar call, or invitation to approach the altar, is practiced as both an extension of the sermon and an embodied response to the Word.[17] During this movement it is common to hear music played or a hymn sung. For example, if the sermon on the Lost Son were to focus on the repentant attitude of the son, the preacher might invite the congregation to respond by approaching the altar as Charlotte Elliott's "Just as I Am" or Matt Goss's "Coming Back" is sung. Again, looking at the topical indexes for themes such as repentance, penitence, or confession might yield such hymns as Charles Wesley's "Depth of Mercy," or a digital search

---

16. Larson, "Seasons of Love."
17. Cherry, *Worship Architect*, 124.

for songs of repentance might yield songs like Robert Robinson's "Come Thou Fount of Every Blessing."

Critical examination of song lyrics is important in making these choices. Using "Come Thou Fount" as an example, the exact words of response may not be obvious just from the title, they may be nested within the song. "Come Thou Fount" is often used as an invocational or opening hymn, but as a hymn of response to a sermon on the Lost Son, the call is in the verse that says, "O to grace how great a debtor daily I'm constrained to be; let thy goodness like a fetter bind my wandering heart to thee. Prone to wander, Lord, I feel it, prone to leave the God I love. Here's my heart, O take and seal it, seal it for thy courts above."[18] For a youth group or a congregation into rock repertoire, the refrain of Bon Jovi's song "Who Says You Can't Go Home" might be more fitting than a hymn:

> Who says you can't go home? There's only one place they call me one of their own. Just a hometown boy born a rolling stone. Who says you can't go home? Who says you can't go back? I been all around the world, and as a matter of fact there's only one place left I want to go. Who says you can't go home?[19]

The youthful congregation may sing this, but if not, the song can serve as a moment of response as it is sung or played by a band.

If a song supports the sermon's function and is familiar to the congregation, such synergy extends the sermon, taking it from the head to the heart to the hands and feet of the listeners. In selecting a song of response, important questions to ask are:

- Does the song support what the preacher hopes the sermon might do?
- Does it give the singers an opportunity to respond to the Word?
- Is there a need to be selective about which verses or parts of the song function best?

18. Robinson, "Come Thou Fount."
19. Bon Jovi and Sambora, "Who Says You Can't Go Home."

- Is there a phrase from this song that can be woven into the ending of the sermon?
- Does it connect with the singers at the heart level? Has it been sung enough times before that some or most know it by heart?

EXAMPLE—"CALLED AND CALLED OUT," CATHERINE E. WILLIAMS, PREACHER

I was invited to be part of a sermon series titled "Who and Whose We Are." Series preachers were asked to consider a narrative approach to our sermons that included our own stories. I chose two texts for my sermon titled "Called and Called Out," Matthew 4:18–20 and John 21:15–19. Both recount call stories where Jesus said to Peter, "Follow me." The sermonic claim of these two texts centered around what a call to follow Jesus might look like and the kind of identity into which that call invites us. The focus statement read, "God's call comes to each of us at various times and in various ways; through it we find identity and affinity." I hoped the sermon would function to inspire and/or challenge us to hear and heed God's call to us as individuals and as a congregation of called-out ones.

Through email and phone conversations, the church's worship pastor and I talked through the initial idea for the sermon and some possible congregational selections for both services. The church has an early Sunday service with contemporary praise-and-worship style music accompanied by a full band, and a later service that uses traditional hymns, a choir, and an organ. This example is based on the contemporary service.

As preacher and musician, we laid out the musical options, which included "Oceans" (Crocker, Houston, and Lighthelm), "Spirit of the Living God" (Sooter and Fieldes), "Gather Us In" (Haugen), "The Summons" (Bell), and "Pues Si Vivimos" (Anon. and Escamilla). Merits and demerits of each song touched on aspects such as how well the congregation knew it, which parts of the song would be most useful, which would point to the sermon's focus, and which would express its function. And since this was too much music for the typical congregational opening set of two songs, we had to determine if and how to best use the other selections. Over the course of phone conversations and email exchanges, ideas flowed back and forth from preacher to musician as one's thoughts challenged, changed, or affirmed the thoughts of the other. Jointly, we were able to clarify the tone of the sermon, the tenor of the service, the placement of the music, and the way this all would fit best within the overall sermon series.

In the end, the two-piece congregational set turned out to be Vertical Worship's "Spirit of the Living God" and Haugen's "Gather Us In," both well known to the congregation. "Spirit of the Living God" proclaimed the singers' commitment to listening for God's call: "We only want to hear your voice, we're hanging on every word . . . come and speak to us, oh Lord."[20] "Gather Us In" functioned nicely as an opening, gathering piece and equally well as an orientation to the sermon's focus: "Call to us now, and we shall awaken, we shall arise at the sound of our name."[21] It also set this service within the frame of the entire "Who and Whose We Are" series with its lyrics of "call us anew to be salt for the earth" (identity) and "gather us in and make us your own" (affinity). By the end of this song-set the congregation had been oriented to listening for God's call. They had also established a sense of identity as those called by God and a sense of affinity as being the gathered, called-out people of God.

We used fragments of the remaining musical selections, sprinkling them throughout the service in a variety of ways. The opening lyrics of "Oceans"—"You call me out upon the waters"[22]—were used as the call to worship. The refrain of "Pues Si Vivimos"—"We belong to God, we belong to God"[23]—was the sung congregational response within the litany-shaped prayers of the people. The lyrics

20. Sooter and Fieldes, "Spirit of the Living God."
21. Haugen, "Gather Us In," 54.
22. Houston, Crocker, and Lighthelm, "Oceans (Where Feet May Fail)."
23. Anon., "Pues Si Vivimos," 356.

of "The Summons" were woven into the Eucharistic prayer of confession and words of assurance:

> **Leader**: Hear the good news; nothing can separate us from the love of God.
>
> **People**: We go in God's company always and everywhere.

As a closing song of response, "The Summons" reinforced and proclaimed my hoped-for outcome—to inspire and/or challenge us to hear and heed God's call to us as individuals and as a congregation of called-out ones. Themes of identity (the called) and affinity (the called-out ones) permeate this hymn. The opening question, "Will you come and follow me?" is reiterated relentlessly over the course of four stanzas. By the time the fifth stanza comes around the response seems organic to this moment of interrogative proclamation—this voice of God that people declared earlier they would hang on every word. The organic response is "yes"— "Lord, your summons echoes true when you but call my name. Let me turn and follow you and never be the same. In your company I'll go, where your love and footsteps show. Thus I'll move and live and grow in you and you in me."[24] Although the first-person pronoun of the response is in the singular, the act of singing the hymn congregationally transforms this into the collective "yes" of the called-out ones. From start to finish this service was an act of proclamation within the dialogical, call-and-response liturgy of a worship service. The songs before the sermon were chosen for their ability to orient the singers toward the sermon's focus. The closing song gave the listeners an opportunity to declare their intent to follow Christ.

---

24. Bell, "Summons."

Preaching and Music

PASTOR-MUSICIAN TALKING POINTS

The Tune

As they evaluate possible musical selections that frame and co-proclaim with the sermon, pastors and musicians may begin with two criteria: the words and the tune. Does the tune register at the levels of head and heart? Another way of asking is, does it get to the heart through its intellectual appeal, or does it get to the intellect through its emotive appeal? Some congregations may prefer one approach over the other; that information is important enough to factor into the musical options. A tune that appeals to the head will have interest and logical flow. One might consider that ANTIOCH, to which we sing the Christmas classic "Joy to the World," has such an intellectual appeal; musically it is logical, orderly, and conceptually interesting.

A tune that appeals to the heart has what writers call a hook—a musical or lyrical phrase people find themselves singing or humming after they go home. One might consider MUELLER, to which we sing the other Christmas classic "Away in a Manger," a song with heart appeal. It is a lullaby, after all, meant to bring calm to the body and impart peace to the soul. To one group the strict, orderly movement of ANTIOCH may feel constraining, while another group may consider MUELLER too saccharine for their taste. The discerning pastor and musician select tunes with their congregation in mind. And if all of this sounds like some unimportant technicality, try exchanging tunes and lyrics between "Joy to the World" and "Amazing Grace." The poetry of both hymns is written in common meter, with a repeat of the last line in the carol. How does that exchange feel? Many would consider that tune exchange a mismatch. The right tune matters.

A pastor may discover a hymn whose words are just perfect—they resonate closely with the sermon. But the tune might be a problem. If the tune is not appealing but the words are, this can diminish the effectiveness of the song. Here is where the musician may suggest another song or another more familiar tune that matches the metrical pattern and ethos of the lyrics. This is also

Framing the Sermon

where a hymnal's metrical index becomes useful. The following information may begin to sound technical, but in many of my classes worship students and preachers alike have found this helpful and enlightening.

Metrical indexes at the back of hymnals indicate the rhythmic pattern of the lyrics. In most hymnals you will see this pattern represented by numbers below the hymn, along with author and date information. If we compare those numbers at the bottom of the hymn page with the metrical index at the back of the hymnal, we may find several tunes to which any hymn with that metrical pattern can be sung. For example, the poetry of "Away in a Manger" has a 11.11.11.11 meter. Turning to the hymnal's metrical index we may find as many as four or five tunes into which those lyrics can fit, among them FOUNDATION—"How Firm a Foundation"—and ST. DENIO—"Immortal, Invisible, God Only Wise." Neither of those two might be the best fit for "Away in a Manger," a lullaby after all, but CRADLE SONG would be perfect. That is the tune congregations in Canada and Great Britain most prefer for this Christmas carol; it also has the gentle, soothing feel of a lullaby. All this to say there are options for using familiar tunes for unfamiliar texts. These options require the thoughtful wisdom that emerges from collaborative conversations between pastor and musician.

The Words

Words matter. In matters of faith words express what we believe through creeds, scriptures, and songs; words inspire and give us hope through sermons and prayers; and words convey our thoughts and feelings through the songs we sing. One hymn writer reminds us, "Worship is more than words, and yet words bear much of the burden of interpreting the meaning of our actions, evoking our faith, and expressing our theology."[25] In this remarkable chapter titled "Vivid Words for Worship," Ruth Duck

---

25. Duck, *Worship for the Whole People of God*, 105.

wisely guides the reader in choosing excellent words for worship, expanding liturgical language to honor all of God's people, and developing mindfulness of how we name God in worship. When choosing songs that expand the sermon's reach, pastor and musician may face some hard choices. One question I hear often is, "What if the song contains verses or a refrain or bridge that work perfectly but other parts miss the mark theologically?" Wisdom guides us to be selective in that case. Pastor and musician can discuss which verses will work best. In our earlier example of "Come Thou Fount," we saw how fitting the final verse was for that specific sermon. In other instances, pastor and musician may find a simple refrain that does the work—"we belong to God, we belong to God." When using older hymns in the public domain we often encounter troubling language that can be altered since these texts are no longer governed by copyright laws. This is one talking point between pastor and musician where conversations can produce a fertile cross-pollination of musicianship and theology for the sake of sound proclamation and spiritual formation.

Expanding the Playlist

Liturgical frustration can occur over the limited number of songs used by a congregation over a yearly cycle, especially when compared to the five, six, or seven hundred hymns contained within a hymnal or an online musical database. John Bell wisely warns, "For many people, the old songs are the best ones. The simple but inarticulated [sic] truth is that they have accrued to them a canon of sacred memories and associations. The new items, as yet unknown, have no pedigree of familiarity and fondness."[26] When pastors and musicians find themselves repeatedly coming up short on suitable musical selections to frame the sermon, what better time to brainstorm ways to expand the congregational repertoire?

Ideally, the canon of songs sung by the congregation needs to include music that aligns with the range of the congregation's

---

26. Bell, *Singing Thing*, 43.

beliefs, challenges them toward spiritual growth, proclaims the whole gospel found in Old and New Testaments, and reinforces the church's mission. Yet congregations love the music they love to sing because of enduring associations they have developed with these songs over time. Some of these associations are on the cognitive level, others are on the affective level. This is why in introducing new music we look for a way to make this intellectual-emotive connection right away. The intellectual connection is facilitated by a strong, well-worded text and a tune that matches the strength and cogency of the words. The heart connection may come through the song's association with a meaningful occasion—such as "On Eagle's Wings" at a grandmother's funeral—or through learning the backstory of the hymn—such as the moving account of Horatio Spafford's family tragedy that led to the writing of "It Is Well with My Soul." Here are a few approaches pastor and musician can employ to increase a congregation's repertoire.

A new song may be introduced by a soloist or ensemble (praise team) singing the first verse, then inviting the congregation to join in the following verses. This works best with an intuitive melody that falls within a singable range, pitched in a comfortable congregational key.

If the church has a choir, it helps to have the choir learn the song so they can provide strong leadership in introducing the song. A choir is vital if the melody is moderately difficult but well worth learning, or if the song is wordy but with words well worth singing.

A song leader can teach a new song in a call and response fashion, where the leader sings one line and the people echo. This works well with a song that has a refrain. The people can learn the refrain first and let the leader sing the verses. This method leads to incremental confidence in learning new material. It also helps if that new song is sung two weeks in succession, a decision that relies on the wisdom of the worship planners.

In some smaller congregations that may not have a choir but have video screening ability, the pastor may play a video of the song sung in a key manageable for a congregation. This calls for streaming permission, especially if the services are live streamed, but it affords musical access. If the video is of good quality visually and musically, it provides inspiration to venture into something new.

If a church has handbells or capable instrumentalists, the song may be played as a prelude or offertory prior to being introduced. This instrumental rendition may increase the emotive value of the song by the time the congregation sings it.

Depending upon the size of the congregation, the musician may do a brief preview or rehearsal of the song prior to the start of worship. Using whatever voices are present before the service starts, the musician may engage them as the core group that will help the rest of the congregation sing this new song later in the service. This may also be the time to provide some backstory to the song, information that can also be printed in the bulletin.

If the poetic meter of the new song is common enough, the metrical index of the hymnal may provide alternative tunes for the new hymn text. Using a tune that is more familiar to the congregation and is well-matched with the hymn's message would be an efficient way to introduce a new hymn.

Finally, few methods can match the hymn sing when it comes to introducing new music. A hymn sing is sometimes billed as an event where music lovers gather just to sing their favorites. It can also be organized to do music both old and new. When songs are introduced with their origin stories or biblical allusions, it can deepen the value of favorites and make those critical intellectual and emotional connections with new songs.

Expanding the congregation's song base is critical collaborative work for pastors and church musicians. Not only does it give the preacher more material to work with in expanding the sermon, but a wider base of congregational songs also widens theological understandings. Brian Wren makes a case for this when he cautions against the theological dangers of a narrow repertoire, a theological constraint that ought to be a pastoral red flag. Wren recommends worship planners think about the arc of the service, even the arc of the liturgical year when aiming for variety in the congregation's musical canon. He advises, "If my repertoire is varied, one hymn's individual piety will be balanced by another's social conscience, and I can entrust myself to the viewpoint of the hymn I'm singing now, confident that it will be enriched, corrected, and supplemented by the next hymn I sing and by the hymns I sing next Sunday."[27] This important work of supporting and expanding the congregation's sung proclamation deserves the kind of multi-perspectival approach of collaborative worship planning. Together the pastor and musician ensure that the sermon continues to live long after its pulpit delivery ends. Both need to agree that songs are part of the proclamation of the Word, not just independent elements going their own way. Both need to agree on the value of purposeful selection as opposed to a service that comes across as a liturgical potluck.

CONCLUSION

Having read this chapter, readers may be reflecting on how this practice of framing the sermon has worked for them or for another preacher in a service they attended. The reader may be slowly coming to a new understanding about the role of music in worship, that it is not as benign or inconsequential as some may think. Even if the homiletical concepts of focus and function are not parts of our sermon development process, and we have some other method for determining what the sermon is going to say and do, adopting this framing concept leads us to discover how much and how well music can share the preacher's load, making the proclamation of the Word more expansive, enduring, and engaging.

---

27. Wren, *Praying Twice*, 365.

3

Musicality and Black Preaching

IN THIS CHAPTER WE turn to the practices of African American preaching as we explore a historically venerated variation of our theme. This symbiotic relationship of music and preaching is a hallmark of Black religious history.[1] It would help for us to begin by addressing assumptions regarding what counts as music. Next, I invite the reader to explore with me the concept of attunement, with its roots in the science of acoustics, as a homiletical strategy. The chapter also calls upon musicology, the academic study of music, to help us match several musical terms to phenomena within Black preaching; in this section musicology meets homiletics. This is followed by sample sermons from two exemplars of African American preaching, Rev. Dr. Gina Stewart and Rev. Dr. Frederick Douglass Haynes III. Since singing can preach as compellingly as preaching can sing within the sphere of Black religious musicality, we take a look at Rev. Shirley Caesar's Tiny Desk concert in the NPR series for an example of Black gospel homiletics. The chapter rounds out with conversation touch points between preacher and musician.

1. Raboteau, *Fire in the Bones*, 147.

Musicality and Black Preaching

Any examination of the musicality of Black preaching must first address assumptions about musicality. It would help the curious student of Black preaching to ask, what exactly counts as music? For Africana[2] peoples the answer is not easily translated using musical terms developed by Europeans to describe and analyze their musical arts, which "emphasized the study of music as sound, focusing on elements of structure and technique."[3] Africana understandings of music as a life force transcend the disciplinary codes and categories standard to formalized music theory. Africana music is heard in pitch and timbre; it is also felt in rhythm and movement. In Black life church music tends to be valued in more functional than aesthetic terms, more rooted in life than in entertainment. Notions of beauty and art are often secondary to an organic response to life in community. In other words, the musicality of Black preaching is expressed in everything from the way the preacher breathes, gestures, and moves to the pitches of the preacher's heightened speech, moaned phrases, and sung delivery, to the sonic and unvoiced responses of the listeners.

This degree of musicality in preaching is not readily understood apart from its natural setting, the Black congregation. This chapter assumes the social context within which the musicality of Black preaching flourishes best and is most deeply understood. In the sage words of Kenyatta Gilbert, "When the African American 'chanted sermon' is attempted or examined in academic contexts without regard to the actual preaching habitats from which the 'chanted sermon' arises, not only will context-determined ways of listening be overlooked, but also missed is the aesthetic genius of this preaching style's interconnected dance of Scripture, culture, body, and voice."[4] This goes to say that members of the African diaspora are likely to resonate intuitively with this chapter, and be affirmed as I name explicitly the genius of these practices. For

---

2. As used throughout this chapter, this term captures musical and other cultural sensibilities generally shared by people groups across the African diaspora. I use this term interchangeably with Black and African American.

3. Burnim and Maultsby, *African American Music*, 7.

4. Gilbert, *Journey and Promise*, 21–22.

other readers I have attempted to do some translating work necessary to grasp concepts that lie outside Europeanized codes of music theory.

What is it about Black preaching that makes it distinctive? Answers to that question have been rhetorical, theological, homiletical, pastoral, and sociopolitical—by no means an exclusive list of perspectives. My answer to that question comes from a musical vantage point, which is not to imply that any of the other categories are discrete. In fact, in the cosmology or worldview of Africana peoples one would be hard pressed to find siloed any category of any kind, or any binary approach to life. Preaching and music may be separated and studied as discrete academic disciplines, but in the living of Black life they are not only inseparable; they are also sometimes indistinguishable one from the other.

ATTUNEMENT: A HOMILETICAL STRATEGY

Critical to this fusion of preaching and music in Black worship is the concept of attunement, the process through which two or more elements or people come into accord or alignment. Attunement and such synonyms as harmony and resonance have their home in the discipline of acoustics, a branch of physics that deals with properties of sound. Tuning is what a string or wind player does to create tonal alignment within the instrument. If that instrument is playing with others, tuning between the instruments is also necessary for a harmonious sound. Tuning is also what happens within a radio where a dial or some other control feature is used to search for the right frequencies where a listener can pick up or tune into a radio broadcast. Both kinds of tuning take time, attentiveness, and a good ear. Both kinds of tuning happen in the best of Black preaching—the preacher is in tune with herself and in tune with all the elements at work in sermon creation and delivery, toward the goal of a fine-tuned, compelling experience in which listeners are tuned in rather than tuned out.

Attunement in Black preaching reflects the high value placed on sound in a culture that values orality over literacy in

Musicality and Black Preaching

communication. James Weldon Johnson's "old-time Negro preacher loved the sonorous mouth-filling, ear-filling phrase because it gratified a highly developed sense of sound and rhythm in himself and his hearers."[5] That highly developed sense of sound is a cultural legacy that marks excellence in Black preaching still today. A well-tuned sound coming from a well-tuned preacher is a hallmark of homiletical musicality.

This principle of attunement works on different levels to create synergy between sermon and song, homily and hymn. It begins with the preacher's spiritual attunement to the presence and activity of God's Holy Spirit through spiritual practices of devotional reading of the scriptures and prayer. It is time spent in these practices that gives us the spiritual ears to detect when we are on pitch or in tune. There is no short-circuiting this any more than one can erect a building without a foundation. Tuning is directly related to hearing. The kind of spiritual tuning required for powerful Black preaching calls for a developed sense of hearing, discerning the presence and voice of God. This is because preaching is at its core an act of worship—a means of encounter with the living God.

In his introduction to the compiled volume *Power in the Pulpit: How America's Most Effective Black Preachers Prepare Their Sermons*, Cleophus LaRue notes that each contributing preacher "speaks in some manner of being encountered by God at the outset of the initial stages of sermon development."[6] Charles G. Adams acknowledges, "Prayer is the beginning of my sermon"[7]; Zan Holmes's sermon preparation method begins with "a period of prayer and devotion"[8]; and Carolyn Knight's strategy for preparation is "pray, prepare, pray, preach, and pray!"[9] From novice to

---

5. Johnson, *God's Trombones*, 7.

6. LaRue, *Power in the Pulpit*, 6.

7. See Adams, "Preaching from the Heart and Mind," in LaRue, *Power in the Pulpit*, 13.

8. See Holmes, "Enabling the Word to Happen," in LaRue, *Power in the Pulpit*, 75.

9. See Knight, "Preaching as an Intimate Act," in LaRue, *Power in the Pulpit*, 100.

Preaching and Music

homiletical veteran, this practice of tuning into the divine wavelength is indispensable. It develops the preacher's spiritual tuning fork and sensitizes the preacher's "dial" to locate psychic and spiritual frequencies and wavelengths that matter in the study and in the sanctuary. Spiritual tuning sharpens the preacher's skill for the work of constant attunement required to preach a compelling sermon. This work begins with preachers' ability to tune into themselves, to acknowledge their own need and vulnerability before God.

This work continues with the preacher's hermeneutical attunement to the sermonic scripture text. As do many other Black homileticians, I admonish students to use the lens of their own cultural experience when reading and interpreting scripture. Simmons and Thomas have termed this "existential exegesis."[10] It is essential if the preacher wants to be on the same wavelength with Black listeners. Such alignment contributes to the sermon's authenticity, causing it to land on ears and hearts familiar with weary years and silent tears. In the best of Black preaching the historical and contemporary experiences of the African American community are a critical counterpoint to the stories of the Bible.[11]

Tuning is constant in the moment of delivery, including all that comes before the sermon. Effective preachers do well to tune in the presence and movement of the Holy Spirit in the worship service. Often a sermonic selection—music that precedes the sermon—will facilitate this tuning work by setting the atmosphere. When Alisha Lola Jones talks about the sermonic selection "setting the atmosphere by relating to the message that will be preached,"[12] she is using an idiom preachers and musicians understand. Setting the atmosphere is another way to speak of creating an environment for harmonious connection with the empowering presence of God. It often happens that if the sermonic selection did not help establish a sense of those divine resonances, the preacher may call for another musical number, or begin singing one himself. That

10. Simmons and Thomas, *Preaching with Sacred Fire*, 8.
11. LaRue, *Heart of Black Preaching*, 13–15.
12. Jones, *Flaming?*, 1.

Musicality and Black Preaching

moment of readiness to launch into the sermon calls for spiritual attunement, without which a preacher is out there on their own!

Another critical tuning moment happens at the outset of the sermon's delivery. Introductions to Black sermons are notoriously lengthy because they are frequently moments of fine-tuning rapport—particularly for a guest preacher—between pulpit and pew. The preacher may take their time expressing gratitude for the invitation to preach, voicing appreciation for the relationship between themselves and the resident pastor and congregation, and giving honor to a litany of persons and ultimately God. Resident pastors may also seek in their introductions to create resonance with recent or current events in the congregation or community. These are not empty, time-filling preambles. In these moments of reading the room the preacher is sounding and holding up her tuning fork, listening as it were for the frequency of the hearts and minds before her. Black preaching introductions are necessarily moments of harmonizing, of getting past the static to find the right broadcast frequencies.

When preachers are in the "start low" mode, they are tuning. Although many refer to the moments approaching the sermon's close as "tuning up," experienced preachers know that tuning happens all throughout the sermon. The preacher keeps listening, moment by moment, phrase by phrase, sentence by sentence, to the point where parts of the prepared manuscript may be skipped over because they are now out of tune with the sonic spirituality of the moment. When this connection between the preacher and the divine Spirit is fine-tuning, it is expressed through an intensifying of emotion often signified by a gradual shift in volume, embodiment, and speech or breathing patterns.

These musical expressions—volume, movement, and breath—are themselves creating music in the room, a resonating, vibrating sounding of what James Weldon Johnson calls harmonies of liberty[13]—the freedom of preacher, Spirit, and people. Congregational responses from "Amen" to "Glory Hallelujah" are

---

13. Johnson and Johnson, *Lift Every Voice and Sing*.

significant indicators of resonance and alignment.[14] They indicate levels at which preacher, congregation, and Spirit are coming into accord. Musicians are also part of this tuning. Some preachers have a tonal key where their voices naturally land once the shift from heightened speech to intoned preaching happens. Some preachers may indicate this key to the musicians, others may intuitively find it and expect the musician to quickly come along; the attuned musician is ever ready. This inflection point has been called "tuning up"; the sermon may now be moving steadily toward the celebration or close.

At this stage, attunement between musicians and preacher now enriches and enlivens the musical tenor of the sermon as it closes. It is normal in these ending moments for the sermon to segue into congregational song. This may be a musical number preselected by a preacher who is in tune with the congregational repertoire, especially their heart songs—the ones they can sing by heart and that minister to them deeply at heart level. The song may also rise up from a lyrical fragment used in the sermon or something that occurred to the preacher in a moment of improvisation. Attentive, attuned musicians determine whether this lyrical fragment is a passing mention or a direction in which the wind of the Spirit is blowing. Whatever the nature or source of the song, it is the vehicle that takes the sermon home to its resting place in the hearts and lives of listeners—a high, harmonious moment where vibrations of the Spirit fill the room with sound played by instruments human, musical, and celestial.

This final moment of tuning may be at fortissimo level as just described. It may also be a different response to the "assurance of grace"[15] just heard. Whatever the mode or affect of the ending, a strong sermon will close tunefully connected to the people and the Spirit in that moment of God's Word going forth. At the core of

---

14. Crawford, *Hum*, 15.

15. Thomas, *They Like to Never Quit*, 17–18. In Thomas's homiletical theory celebration is an organic response to the good news of the assurance of grace, not merely a customary sermonic ending, unrelated to what came before.

every compelling Black sermon is attunement from preparation to delivery, from introduction to closing.

MUSICOLOGY MEETS HOMILETICS

What counts as music in Black preaching? Homileticians and musicologists offer us a smorgasbord of answers that use musical and rhetorical terminology. Teresa Fry Brown uses categories of "linguistic intonation, ebb and flow, call and response, inflection and physicality," as well as "intonation, rhythm and repetition."[16] Jon Michael Spencer analyzes the correlation between Black preaching and spirituals using categories of melody, rhythm, call and response, harmony, counterpoint, form, and improvisation.[17] From Samuel Floyd's musicological analysis we retrieve terms such as "calls, cries, and hollers; hums, moans, groans, grunts, vocables; interjections and punctuations; and timbral distortions of various kinds."[18] This sampling of terminology offered by scholars of Africana orality already begins to broaden standard ideas of what counts as music. These musical idioms of Black preaching are the cultural legacy of regional African oral traditions, where storytelling was a fine art practiced by griots, "West African artisans of the word,"[19] whose multiple roles included keeping the community informed and connected. Because this is a heritage that calls upon cultural memory, it cannot be appropriately taught by homileticians foreign to Africana culture. Most if not all Black homileticians would say this way of preaching is primarily "caught" through cultural apprenticeship rather than taught through classes and courses.

Yet, classes and courses are important to musicology, the study of music which gives us nomenclature for what we hear and experience in music-making. What follows is my effort at

---

16. Brown, *Delivering the Sermon*, 37.
17. Spencer, *Sacred Symphony*, 1–16.
18. Floyd, *Power of Black Music*, 6.
19. Hale, *Griots and Griottes*, 1.

correlating rudimentary musical terminology with the phenomenon of Black preaching. I provide a partial glossary of terms preachers and scholars have used to name and describe musical elements that correlate with traditional Black sermons. Some of these terms resist neat definition or description. Some of them overlap in practice. I will do my best for the sake of students and pastors both native and foreign to Black homiletics, who would benefit from the following curated glossary of terms.

Movements/Moves

David Buttrick's homiletical moves and structures have become a staple in homiletical theory,[20] yet long before Buttrick, African American preaching was characterized by a sequence of moves. A large-scale orchestral work provides a helpful musical comparison. Most symphonies have three or four movements differentiated by style or tempo. Sometimes there is a pause between movements, other times they shift seamlessly one into the next. Often the final movement is the most exciting or dramatic, such as Beethoven's Ninth, which ends with the driving, roof-raising choral number, "Ode to Joy." Symphonic movements take the attentive listener on a journey, as do the moves in a traditional African American sermon. Four commonly identified Black sermonic moves—start low, go slow, climb higher, strike fire—signify shifts that mark the sermon's journey from start to finish.[21] Occasionally a preacher will add a final movement of "cool down" to recap the sermon's theme and main points. This "cool down" ensures that the congregation's ecstatic, embodied responses do not eclipse the reason for the celebration. Moves are one way to organize a sermon's structure; they can provide memory prompts for the preacher who prefers to preach from an outline rather than a fully written manuscript.

20. Buttrick, *Homiletic*, 23–24.
21. See Turner, "Musicality of Black Preaching," in Childers and Schmit, *Performance in Preaching*, 191.

Musicality and Black Preaching

Tempo

The traditional African American sermon begins slowly. This is the tempo of the introduction, which often includes the reading of the Scripture text. In these introductory moments the preacher is tuning in to the congregation's frequencies. This connection is important. The sermon may have been written in full or conceived in outline form by the preacher, but for the delivery to have impact and meaning the congregation must be engaged and actively involved. If the preacher is a guest, he goes even slower than normal here as he gets a reading on the congregational "vibe." Even if this is the preacher's flock, he still needs to read where they are *today*. These sermonic introductions are comparable to the players in an orchestra tuning their instruments before the piece begins. The preacher may sound as eclectic or unfocused as an orchestra does in those moments when different instruments not only tune to the oboe but play little snatches of music. The preacher may honor the host and express gratitude for the invitation to preach. They may give an account of a recent event in their lives that may or may not have bearing on their sermon, all toward building rapport and establishing rhetorical *ethos* in the moment. Homiletical musicality here is all about tuning—about finding and matching the congregation's wavelength. Even in the shortest sermons or homilies, even in delivering the "same" sermon to the eleven o'clock crowd as preached to the eight o'clock crowd, this tuning is crucial to audience engagement and response.

Antiphony

Audience engagement in Black preaching finds its counterpart in this ancient musical practice where two groups of singers sing in turn, one group answering the other. If you have heard monks or priests singing antiphonally, you know this calling and responding to each other is predictable based on the structure of the chant. While medieval antiphonal chanting can be gentle and smooth, there are Africana versions of such musicality that are rhythmic, energetic, and spontaneous. It is this spontaneity that distinguishes the antiphonal nature of Black proclamation in both preaching and singing. The call can arise from any source; so can the response. The preacher may call and the organ respond, the people may call and the preacher respond, or the organ or any other musical instrument may call and the preacher respond. Musicologists have observed that "the statement and answer sometimes overlap."[22] Such is the polyrhythmic nature of Africana musical performance practice; there is no need to wait until the call has ended before giving a response, and vice versa. This happens so organically in Black preaching and music, most involved don't conceive of what they are doing in musical terms. But this practice marks inspired Black preaching at its height—the good news is being collaboratively produced and proclaimed.

Volume

Skilled preachers use this musical dynamic to employ variety in expression and create levels of intensity that match sermonic content. Uncontrolled fervor is unhelpful—even counterproductive—when it results in a sustained fortissimo or maximum volume early in the sermon, often prompted by the preacher's anxiety. Better to save the fullest volume for the sermon's close. More rhetorically effective is the purposeful use of crescendo—gradual increase in volume—and decrescendo—gradual decrease in volume—within sermonic moves. It gives the sermon a more organic feel and suggests the sermon is breathing naturally. The skilled preacher knows how to harness the timing of loud and soft delivery to match the sermon's content. Attuned to the moment, they know when and for how long to preach at full volume and when an intense whisper would communicate just as effectively. For the attuned preacher, the body's wisdom can be a guide through these variations in volume. Remember that the vocal cords are the preacher's instrument; we do well to play them skillfully, even in moments of excitement.

---

22. Burnim and Maultsby, *African American Music*, 8.

Musicality and Black Preaching

Even though some may equate volume with anointing, wise is the preacher who will not let the energy of the anointing drive them to damage their vocal instrument.

Repetition

Musically, repetition facilitates a composer's intent to emphasize an idea or a theme. In preaching, repetition as a rhetorical device not only contributes to the musicality of the sermon; it also invites the audience into a musical way of listening.[23] Skilled use of repetition reinforces key ideas, drives home the sermon's point, invites audience participation, adds memorability to the sermon, creates space for improvisation, and builds momentum that sustains listener engagement. In his remarkable analysis of Martin Luther King Jr.'s preaching Lischer notes how King's use of repetition could skillfully amplify a single idea through copiousness and intensification.[24] Repetition also happens in the sermon when the preacher returns to a phrase or idea much like how a song finds its way back to a refrain at the end of a verse. This device enhances the memorability of the sermon in much the same way as when the refrain comes more readily to mind than the verses when one is trying to recall a song. To anyone skeptical of repetition in preaching I draw your attention to the psalms we preach. This is a classic feature of poetry and music: "Praise him, all his angels; praise him, all his host! Praise him, sun and moon; praise him all you shining stars!"[25] Repetition partners well with other musical elements such as volume, rhythm, and cadence, to help an audience tune in rather than tune out.

23. Shelley, *Healing for the Soul*, 64.
24. Lischer, *Preacher King*, 129.
25. Psalm 148:2–30.

Preaching and Music

Pacing

I use this term to refer to how the phrases in music are timed and the spacing between one phrase and the next. In preaching this is closely related to tempo. Once past the introduction, pacing begins to quicken gradually—*poco a poco*—as the preacher moves ever closer to that finely tuned sweet spot. The preacher has gained and kept the attention of the listeners, who, by their audible or body language, have begun to give instructive feedback. Sermonic phrases begin to sound pleasingly contoured; tones may be extended for emphasis; pauses between sentences become shorter; volume is increasing gradually; and wordplay is livelier. Pace and intensity match the degree to which the preacher is in tune with all the elements at play in this moment of sermon delivery. Pacing that responds to sermonic shifts in content and intensity contributes to the musicality of the sermon by giving it artistic shape and form.

Pauses and Silences

Musical composers understand the sonic value of rests strategically placed between sounds. Music is happening there, too; the larger work is breathing and alive in these moments. Pauses in Black preaching have many strategic functions, including creating suspense and anticipation.[26] They can also underscore the impact of what was said just before the pause. Often extemporaneous preachers use silence to tune into the moment, to help them discern what next to say. Audience response has made them pause to consider whether they need to stay on the current point just a little while longer or keep the outline/manuscript moving. Crawford's wisdom names this moment as "an opening in the preacher's consciousness through which the musicality of the Spirit breathes so that the musicality of the sermon resonates with living truth."[27] These pauses are often moments when the audience's responses will co-create the sermon with intercalations and responses that

---

26. Crawford, *Hum*, 31.
27. Crawford, *Hum*, 17.

expand meaning beyond the preacher's words: "Well, ain't that the truth!" "Say it again, preacher!" or "I know that's right!" It cannot be overstated how important it is for a sermon to breathe in this way. It is as vital as human breathing. The deeper the breath, the more oxygen can do its clarifying and calming work in the preacher's body. The more intentional and well-timed the pause, the better for listeners to absorb concepts and track with the flow of sermonic thought.

Cadence

Musically, this is how a performer or conductor will phrase or shape the melody. Homiletically, we hear cadence in the preacher's vocal inflection—how she shapes the contours of a sentence to develop a musical flow or rhythm by the way her voice rises and falls. We hear this most often in repeated phrases with rhetorical patterns such as anaphora, in which the same cluster of words begins each phrase or sentence. A cadenced reading of Romans 8:30 may place three points of inflection in each phrase—at the beginning, middle, and end: "And *those* whom he *predestined* he also *called*; and *those* whom he *called* he also *justified*; and *those* whom he *justified* he also *glorified*." The repetition in these phrases already summons the music; the preacher's cadenced inflection shapes the phrase; and volume, intonation and percussive embodiment can all add to produce the cadenced sound. Sometimes the preacher's cadences are intuitive and happen in a moment of improvisation. Wise is the manuscript preacher who plans some of this shaping work around repeated questions, repeated ideas, or other high moments of the sermon's delivery.

Meter

In music, a meter tells the ear how many beats there are in a measure or group of sounds. It generally gives the pulse of the music a pattern that the ear can follow. In preaching, this musical aspect is often most pronounced in those parts of the sermon when the preacher moves through a litany of some sort, sometimes called a roll call. A popular roll call is the way Jesus is revealed in all the books of the Old Testament. "In Genesis he's the . . ., In Exodus he's the . . ., In Leviticus he's the . . ." and so on. In these patterns the ear can pick up a certain number of beats to each phrase, similar to musical beats within a measure; this gives the performance of the sermon structure and energy. In those energetic moments it is not unusual for the drummer, the keyboardist, or the people's responses to begin marking time with the meter of the sermon. In this regard meter is closely related to rhythm.

Rhythm

In music theory rhythm refers to how beats are arranged stylistically. One hears of Latin rhythms or Afro rhythms in which distinctive patterns and syncopation identify a certain ethnic origin. Rhythm is encoded into Africana life, experienced primarily through drumming and dancing; it has been called "perhaps the most important aspect of the preacher's musical art."[28] Rhythm in preaching is also tied to meter and cadence, expressed through many rhetorical devices, including anaphora, alliteration, antiphony, and wordplay. When the preacher's breathing patterns become audible, they may also mark these rhythmic expressions. As the preacher's utterances become rhythmic or when these patterns change, it signals that a shift in energy has taken place or is currently happening. The preacher's rhythmic patterns may also be enhanced by percussive responses from musical instruments or from rhythmic congregational feedback such as claps, calls, shouts, or movements. In Jon Michael Spencer's words, rhythm is "the element that gives black preaching locomotion and momentum."[29] Since rhythm is so interconnected with dance, it should be no

---

28. Rosenberg, *Can These Bones Live?*, 63.
29. Spencer, *Sacred Symphony*, 3.

surprise if the preacher breaks into some coordinated movement, some bodily accompaniment to the sermon's rhetorical rhythms.

Percussive Movement

Percussion instruments are played when they are struck. In the piano, hammers strike strings that vibrate and produce sound. In the drum sound is produced when the player strikes the skin with the hand or a stick. In sermon delivery the preacher may use the pulpit as an instrument, striking it to underscore the impact of words or phrases. Percussive movement may also be through bodily gestures, such as bouncing or tilting forward, that work like musical accents to highlight something important or create a syncopated rhythm. Sounds of clapping, leg slapping, and foot stomping add percussion to the sermon, often as accompaniment to repeated phrases, a roll call of celebrated names, or an extended listing such as when the preacher goes through the books of the Bible or letters of the alphabet, reciting the occurrence of a certain theme. Like the use of volume, percussive movement is ineffective, maybe even distracting, when it occurs steadily or randomly from the start of sermon to the finish. If the preacher has the habit of constant bodily gestures not connected to any musical or rhetorical device in the sermon, he may need to be coached out of that habit, as it may be more related to anxiety than homiletical musicality. In the best of sermonic moments, percussion and movement are bonded partners in Africana musicality. They work to enrich the preacher's delivery, underscoring matters of importance.

Intonation

Scholars have used both chant and tone to describe variations of musical pitch in Black preaching. I prefer the word "intoned" to describe this sonic variation in which the preached word is sung. Chant suggests melodic movement around a limited range of pitches, sometimes as few as two or three tones. This is not what happens when preachers begin to intone the sermon. The melodic range tends to be wider than a chant and resembles the operatic feature called *sprechstimme*, which is a cross between speaking and singing. Indeed, the preacher may move freely back and forth between speech and song, and, depending on the preacher, one may be hard pressed at times to tell the difference. This synergy between preaching and music is powerful and engaging. It also contains another musical feature which I will call syllabic expansion. The corresponding musical term is "melisma," in which the composer or performer stretches out one syllable over several notes. Many popular examples exist; one is Handel's "Hallelujah Chorus." ("And He shall rei-ei-eign, for-e-e-ver and e-e-ver.") Another even more dramatic example is "For Unto Us a Child Is Born," in which the soloist extends the word "born" over sixty-four quickly moving notes. Gospel and pop music singers frequently employ melismas as a way to emphasize the importance of a certain word or sound. This was a hallmark of the late Whitney Houston's style. In African American preaching this happens frequently as the sermon begins to "climb higher," tuning into that musical realm where tones convey a surplus of meaning.[30] When in his mountain top speech of April 3, 1968, Martin Luther King declares, "I've looked over, and I've se-e-e-n the promised land," that intoned syllable captures the very fearlessness with which he faces his future.[31] The homiletic melisma is a way for art and preaching to convey meaning that is otherwise inexpressible. This may or may not segue into some form of "whooping," in which, based on individual style, a preacher may add extra syllables to words or phrases.

Improvisation

Improvisation is a major feature of many forms of music from classical to folk. It is especially stylized in jazz, in which the creativity

---

30. Turner uses this phrase to speak of meaning that transcends rational, human vocabulary in "Musicality of Black Preaching," in Childers and Schmit, *Performance in Preaching*, 200–201.

31. King, "I've Been to the Mountaintop," 42:32.

of the performer is on display, not just to impress, but because the performer by that point has become one with the music and attuned to the moment. Kirk Byron Jones sagely observes, "The music of jazz and gospel preaching share some of the same essential ingredients, which include *sound, story,* and *transcendence*."[32] As the preacher tunes into the audience, particularly their responses to certain ideas, words, or phrases, such feedback becomes an invitation or inspiration to riff on the prevailing idea. Improvisation in enslaved communities birthed the spirituals that allowed our ancestors to transcend their horrific existence. It created the wandering refrains African Americans tacked on to European hymns, "a form of improvisation which infuses a large amount of informality into the worship service."[33] It is improvisation that lures the preacher away from the manuscript when they make a life-related connection that didn't happen in the study. It often comes through divine inspiration as the breath of God blows through the lines of the printed sermon. It gives the sermon buoyancy and immediacy as it seeks to fine-tune resonance with the listening audience. Improvisation is frequently most prolific at the sermon's close, when the title of the sermon or some key phrase may turn into a riff or a homiletical *ostinato*—a continually repeated phrase that drives home the point of the sermon with vigor and vibrancy.

Cadenza or Finale

In European art music, the ending of a piece may happen with an improvisational flourish called a cadenza, most often performed by a solo artist. This is comparable to the fanfare of a sermonic close in some Black preaching traditions. Most times if the preacher has been using a manuscript, that printed sermon is now off to the side as the preacher—now fully attuned to the Spirit, the moment, and the people—is free to follow the divine Wind where it blows. And this is nothing if not a flourish. Full physical animation

32. Jones, *Jazz of Preaching*, 27.
33. Costen, *In Spirit and in Truth*, 54.

accompanies the words; repetition does its richest, deepest work; rhetorical persuasion through pathos is at full force; the volume may be at its loudest; the delivery—whether through intoned or sung words—is sonorous; heaven is communicating to earth the ineffable and the unutterable, beyond the sphere of reason or logic; musical instruments have joined the proclamation; and under the best of circumstances everybody and everything is riding a sermonic tidal wave.

By this point the preacher, if whooping is their practice, is in full musical form. "Whooping is first melody, one that can be identified by the fact that its pitches are logically connected and have prescribed, punctuated rhythms that require certain modulations of the voice, and is often delineated by quasi-metrical phrasings."[34] Such is Martha Simmons's fine academic attempt at describing the indescribable. Numerous other scholars of African American preaching have also made their contributions to noteworthy descriptions of whooping, but the practice remains better experienced than explained.[35] At the height of the sermon's close the whooping preacher is caught up in a sonic euphoria; sounds, words, tones, percussive movement, instruments, voices, and bodies engage in effusive, collaborative sermon production in which the preaching is singing and the music is preaching. This is the musicality of Black preaching in one of its most riveting forms, when even skeptics may find it impossible to remain unmoved by the experience.[36]

In this homiletical finale the preacher often tunes into the hymnic memory and musical soundscape of the congregation to

34. See Simmons, "Whooping," in Simmons and Thomas, *Preaching with Sacred Fire*, 865.

35. Scholarly treatment of whooping can be found in the writings of Martha Simmons (*Preaching with Sacred Fire*), Ashon T. Crawley (*Blackpentecostal Breath*), Evans Crawford (*Hum*), Braxton Shelley (*Healing for the Soul*), and Jon Michael Spencer (*Sacred Symphony*).

36. James Weldon Johnson, recounting his experience listening to an old-time Negro preacher, reports, "I sat fascinated; and more, I was, perhaps against my will, deeply moved; the emotional effect upon me was irresistible" (*God's Trombones*, 5).

heighten the flourish of their close. Here the songwriter's words do what only poetry can do to engage and express the sublime. This tradition of ending with a fitting hymn or thoughtfully selected song is highly significant and effective when it encapsulates in memorable form the sermon's main idea or call to action. This practice "reaffirms the vital importance of the sung word in black religion."[37] It allows the sermon to land more deeply in the hearts of the listeners as they lift up their voices in song, jointly proclaiming God's good news.

SAMPLE SERMONS

The following annotations of two sample sermons would be most instructive when read before and after viewing the sermons. In this way the reader can experience the sermon in "real" time. The corresponding footnotes provide links to these videos.

GINA STEWART: "AN UNCOMPROMISED COMMITMENT"[38]

Dr. Gina M. Stewart is a gifted African American preacher, the pastor of Christ Missionary Baptist Church in Memphis, Tennessee, and a much sought-after itinerant revivalist and preacher to preachers. Stewart preached this sermon in a chapel service on February 4, 2015, at Christian Theological Seminary in Indianapolis, Indiana. The sermon trains a womanist lens on the biblical account of two Egyptian midwives. Shiphrah and Puah, in Stewart's words, "told Pharaoh, 'No!' so Moses could tell God, 'Yes!'" The biblical narrative from which she is preaching is found in Exodus 1:15–22.

If we outlined Stewart's sermon, we could plot the four moves: start low, go slow, climb higher, strike fire. However, we

---

37. LaRue, *Power in the Pulpit*, 8.

38. Stewart, "Uncompromised Commitment." https://www.youtube.com/watch?v=47dx0ffCdSM.

would make two modifications. Whereas the first two moves are fairly discrete, the third move is more nuanced. Her climbing higher is a sequence of steps that take the sermon higher in terms of emotive, theological, and existential crescendo. Second, there is a fifth move in this sermon, typical of Stewart and other African American preaching exemplars. On the heels of the heightened close is a recapitulation that happens either through an intentional decrescendo or through a prayer; Stewart uses both methods at the end. The purpose of this fifth move is to ensure that the excitement of celebrating the good news has not in fact eclipsed this good news or the sermon's call to action.

Her opening starts low. Although there is no lack of interpretive nuance or musical undulation in her voice as she reads the narrative, this is the lowest level of volume, pitch, or intensity in the entire sermon. As the preacher transitions from the scripture to giving her title to delivering the first lines, she goes slowly. There are varying degrees of slow in the launching of African American sermons, and much depends on how much time the preacher has within the context of the entire service. Because this is a chapel service whose length is somewhere around forty to fifty minutes, the preacher would have somewhere between fifteen and twenty minutes to deliver the Word—not a whole lot of time for a drawn-out introduction. In this case, whether due to the editing out of the introduction in the video, or for reasons of time expediency, this delivery skips the traditional relaxed opening for which Black preaching is known. Stewart delves right into the sermon manuscript as she speaks about women in the narratives of Scripture often being cast as extras or maybe as supporting roles, but rarely ever the main characters. At this her audience gives immediate feedback as the antiphonal work of call and response begins.

Stewart continues slowly, but this second move is relatively short as it is clear from audience engagement that they have caught the sermon's ironic motif and are ready to help the preacher on her climb to higher levels of volume, pitch, and intensity. The climb is slow. The sentences are short. Stewart carefully lays bare the patriarchal assumptions underlying the story, which she deftly identifies as still existing today. Her contemporary analog ends with the one direct musical reference in this sermon, the James Brown hit "It's a Man's World." What the apt reference to Brown's song does for this sermon is to interlock the world of the biblical text with the contemporary world. Music, even an unsung reference to a song, will often function as an analogy that makes the sermon's point with greater clarity and immediacy than any well-reasoned explication. Furthermore, musical references create space for individual interpretation and application. The hearer's association with the song becomes an interpretive lens. This is neither a good nor bad thing in itself; the same thing can happen with any imagery or illustration the preacher uses to clarify a point.

Returning to the biblical narrative, Stewart's spiral climb gradually crescendos as she draws attention to the book of Exodus, dominated by male characters, yet very early it turns on the actions of the "extras" in the story—the women. The antiphony in the room indicates increasing levels of energy and intensity as Stewart lists the five women without whom there would be no Moses story.

Gifted storyteller that she is, Stewart narrows the focus to the characters of the two midwives. Her bodily animation gradually becomes percussive as she accentuates key words with a head nod or upper body tilt. Her inhalation becomes more pronounced, signifying a growing attunement to the presence of the Holy Spirit and the collective human energy. The "climb higher" phase proceeds in small shifts as the preacher moves through critical moments in the sermon's journey. When Stewart gets to the moment where she speaks of Pharaoh's government administration in terms her listeners can understand, her passion for social justice is signified by another level of intensity.

Musically the sermon slips into another crescendo with more pronounced bodily accentuation of key words and ideas, as in when the preacher's hands and head seem to "conduct" her words: "The threat of the loss of control causes him to speculate and make moves and imagine what life would be like—Lord, help me here!— if these Hebrew boys grow up to be strong and rise up against us!"

Preaching and Music

The intercalation "Lord help me here" is a sure sign of climbing higher; the preacher is beginning to feel the increasing energy in her body and in the room, and she utters a quick prayer for precise spiritual tuning as the homiletical crescendo increases.

Improvisation or going off script for Stewart is often a sign of attunement. Just as sometimes an instrument will need tuning after being played for some time, sometimes a manuscript preacher will experience a tweaking of the written sermon mid-delivery. Such a tuning moment happens for Stewart as she talks about the working conditions under which Pharaoh held the Hebrew slaves. "Despite the forced labor, despite the unreasonable expectation to make bricks without straw, with low wages, no wages, no benefits, the Hebrews continued to multiply." She looks up from her script. "It's an amazing thing how the thing that was intended to break you often makes you. It's an amazing thing how the very thing intended to take you out often gives you strength to overcome." The audience responds with applause. This brief moment of improvisation affords attunement to the room; a word of encouragement blended with astute critique of African American history strikes a resonant note in the atmosphere as the sermon continues its climb.

The metrical rhythms of the sermon become more pronounced with repeated instances of anaphora, beginning a series of sentences with the same words. "What will the oppressed do if they become too many and have access to power? What will the rich do if the poor keep asking for more? What will the women do if we release them and allow them to share in leadership? What will Blacks do if we really give them the right to vote? What will immigrants do if we grant them the privilege of citizenship?" In this case, the repetition at the beginning of each question builds momentum and intensity, each one taking the sermon one more step upward. The last step turns the spotlight back to the midwives who feared God. They are not only pivotal to the biblical narrative, but they are also pivotal to Stewart's sermon as she heads steadily toward the close.

Even with its forward momentum there is a slight decrescendo, almost like a long jumper taking a few steps back before

Musicality and Black Preaching

breaking into that focused run, or like a driver taking her foot off the accelerator to engage the gear shift. This musical dip in flow and energy allows what follows to have even greater impact. It is the courage of the midwives in the face of imperial power that generates not just another crescendo but an accelerando, an increase in the rhetorical tempo. "But the midwives—somebody say the midwives—were operating out of a moral commitment." Stewart is about to frame the vocation/calling of the midwives in specific terms: those who bring life, not death. The preacher is setting up the function of the sermon here as she outlines in a variety of ways the continuing work of this life-giving vocation today, which we are about to learn is our vocation, too. Inviting the audience to say "the midwives" is not a benign call and response moment, or a filler to keep people attentive. The preacher's call for this response is to have that word "midwives" imprinted upon and embedded within the hearts of her listeners through embodiment. Antiphony, especially when guided by the preacher, can drive home the point through participation. While some preachers ask the audience to repeat words or phrases as a habit, sometimes to the point of annoyance, Stewart uses guided antiphony strategically. The words she asks us to repeat are key to the outcome of her sermon.

Repetition is a key feature of Stewart's preaching. She has the gift of saying the same thing several times but with different nuance each time. The notion of women being extras and marginal in the story returns repeatedly throughout the sermon, like a song's refrain or hook. The work of midwives to bring life rather than death is reiterated with increasing energy as the sermon draws to its close. The notion of commitment to the work of justice pops through the sermon's fabric like a bright, reappearing thread. She also uses anaphora to say the same thing in different ways. "Their daily work, their daily routine, what they woke up to do in the morning was to help bring new life into the world." Anaphora sometimes switches to epistrophe, in which, instead of the repeated phrase coming at the beginning of a phrase, it comes at the end, as in the switch from "when we act as a midwife we roll up our sleeves . . . when we act as a midwife we step off the sidelines" to "when we see something happening that is unjust and speak up, we're acting like a midwife, every time we tutor a child, whenever we address literacy . . . we're acting like a midwife." Stewart is approaching the grand finale, the sermon's cadenza. The detailed, pragmatic examples are increasingly rhythmic, calling forth equally rhythmic responses from the audience. The cadenced beat of the sermon continues relentlessly into a roll call of names of people and institutions who have acted in the role of midwives. "Thank God for the midwives" becomes thank God for freedom bearers, historically Black colleges and universities, the Student Nonviolent Coordinating Committee, the Southern Christian Leadership Conference, Rainbow PUSH, NAACP, and a number of esteemed organizations and people of prominence within the African American community.

Strike fire! There is full body animation now as each "thank God" is accentuated with a pointed forefinger. Full embodiment includes deep torso bends that punctuate these cadenced phrases. The audience's energy is peaking; they are clapping and responding improvisationally to each phrase. Then the preacher guides their response toward individual reflection. "You ought to stop right now and tell God thank you for every midwife . . . every teacher, coach, librarian, cafeteria manager . . . you ought to thank God for the midwives. I said you ought to thank God, you ought to thank God for the midwives." As people rise to their feet to celebrate this good news, the sound in the room is now orchestral. The sermon is being collaboratively produced as the good news is shared by all. The good news of the Egyptian midwives has now become the good news of the people in the pews.

The preacher approaches the high point of the finale as she reminds the audience of the reason to keep thanking God for the midwives: "Because Pharaoh ain't dead . . . and if we're not careful . . . rather than being helpers we will turn into hurters because power told us to do so. Aaah, but when you fear God." At this point the reach of the sermon has gone deep, the spirit in the air is high, the radius of energy has gone wide, reaching the limits of the room. This is what Black preachers call the close and what music

Musicality and Black Preaching

composers call the grand climax. There is yet one more roll call that brings the co-created sermon to full fortissimo. This roll call begins with the invitation, "Come on and thank God." The sermon's grand finale is an antiphonal celebration of gratitude for another list of midwives—male, female, and institutional—that have meaning to the gathered body. "Why don't you clap your hands and tell God thank you for the midwives. Come on and thank him for Shiphrah and Puah, *come on and thank him* for Fannie Lou Hamer, Mary McLeod Bethune, Miriam and Esther, Sojourner Truth, Betty Shabazz, Barbara Jordan, Martin Luther King, Malcolm X, Mandela, Frank Thomas, Jeremiah Wright, Christian Theological Seminary." The preacher directs the orchestral celebration with her arms and body swinging from side to side as she instructs her audience, "Open your mouth and tell God Thank You!"

The fire has been struck. The preacher is in full conducting mode—"you ought to praise God, you ought to give God glory, you ought to clap your hands all ye people and shout to God with a voice of triumph." Her final instruction is for them to reach out and touch the hand of the person standing next to them. This accentuates and symbolizes the communal character of the moment and the experience. This community has proclaimed together. What began as a solo turned into a concerto and ended with the full orchestra.

There is one final move: the recapitulation or "cool down." This takes place through the post-sermonic prayer as the audience stands hand in hand while the pianist adds affirmation through a chosen song. The preacher begins by thanking God for a vast, unknown host of midwives. In her prayer she continues to guide the audience's response: "I squeeze my neighbor's hand now in thanks for their life, in thanks for their ministry, in thanks for their assignment." Stewart prays for strength to claim and reclaim our moral authority. The prayer is an extension of the sermon: "We know that whenever human authority conflicts with your authority laws have already been broken." Antiphony continues throughout the prayer as people respond in the pauses between phrases and sentences. Words and phrases from the sermon populate the prayer. The preacher, although not quite returned to the low level of volume or intensity of the beginning, has turned down the dial considerably so that minds can engage what hearts and bodies did moments earlier.

Stewart does not sing or invite people to sing in this musical sermon. Once the preacher closes her electronic device, a musician approaches the piano and begins playing softly "I Don't Feel No Ways Tired." Yet there is much music to be heard in the rhythm of cadenced phrases, the percussive movement providing musical accents, the antiphony both guided and spontaneous, the repetition through use of rhetorical patterns, the hand clapping, and the dynamic use of volume, pauses, and tempo. As does most Black preaching, Stewart's sermon invites us to recalibrate our understanding of what counts as music.

FREDERICK DOUGLASS HAYNES III—"AND IF YOU DON'T KNOW, NOW YOU KNOW"[39]

Frederick Douglass Haynes III is the senior pastor at Friendship West Baptist Church in Dallas, Texas. He is also a much sought-after itinerant revivalist. I was fortunate to be present as he preached this sermon at the revival service held October 25, 2023, at Eastern Star Church, Indianapolis, Indiana. Haynes has done revivals at this congregation for the past thirty years. The musicality of this sermon is in its title, in snatches of hymns and popular song lyrics that either illustrate the preacher's point or express what he is trying to say in a way that registers deeply. Musicality also comes through the preacher's spoken word style of delivery.[40]

Haynes opens his sermon with a prayer, into which are seamlessly woven the lyrics of three hymns. The purpose of this prayer

---

39. Haynes, "If You Don't Know." https://www.youtube.com/watch?v=2lA1RPFYFwI.

40. The Poetry Foundation defines spoken word as "a broad designation for poetry intended for performance that can encompass or contain elements of rap, hip-hop, storytelling, theater, and jazz, rock, blues, and folk music." See "Spoken Word."

Musicality and Black Preaching

is to both center the preacher in a posture of receptivity to the Spirit and to attune his own spirit to the task at hand. In just under three minutes this prayer uses vocabulary from Edith Cherry's "O to Be Kept by Jesus," Andrae Crouch's "We Need to Hear From You," and Adelaide Potter's "Have Thine Own Way, Lord." These hymn fragments give liturgical context to what is about to happen. Preaching is an act of worship, connected closely to everything else that happens around it in the context of a service; this includes the music and the prayers. This music-infused, pre-sermonic prayer demonstrates the wholistic nature of the Black sermon and its organic connection to prayer and song. As Wyatt Tee Walker so astutely noted in his 1983 Hampton lecture, preaching, praying, and singing are the primary ingredients of Black worship, and in each one you will find elements of the other.[41]

The sermon owes its title to the lyrics of a hip-hop song. Preachers of all cultures take the titles of their sermons from songs. This often has the effect of creating a bond between preacher and audience. To the listener familiar with the song, the sermon's title extends an invitation to enter the sermon through this musical door. Haynes is careful to explain that his sermon title, "And If You Don't Know, Now You Know," is borrowed from B.I.G.'s rap "Juicy." Later in the sermon, Haynes does a close analysis of the song, but already, by use of this popular line from "Juicy," he has established a strong *ethos* or credibility with the rap and hip-hop enthusiasts in the crowd.

The sermon's focus is on Judas's act of betrayal as recorded in John 18:1–11. The preacher again draws on the potency of Black popular music to express the pain of betrayal. This time he calls the O'Jays to bear witness through their song "Backstabbers." The lineup of the sermon's musical witnesses also includes the rapper Jay-Z, who popularized the famous lines, "Don't tell me what was said about me, tell me why they felt so comfortable saying it to you." These musical witnesses are part of the preacher's attempt to establish rapport with his audience. Their responses indicate a strong level of attunement in the room.

41. Walker, *Soul of Black Worship*, 3.

Preaching and Music

Jay-Z's commentary on Martin Luther King works for Haynes as the preacher relates the irony of King being betrayed by another Black man who happened to be on the balcony of the Lorraine hotel in Memphis when King was assassinated. Haynes introduces this move in his sermon with Jay-Z's lyrics: "Everybody want to be the king til shots ring. You laying on a balcony with holes in your dream."[42] Following musically is Lauryn Hill, who sings about the kind of social control exercised by empires in her song "Black Rage." These lyrical examples amplify the poignancy of Judas's actions and his complicity with the Roman Empire in betraying Jesus, who had included Judas in his inner circle of friends.

Haynes's musicality turns to extensive use of anaphora. As he recounts instances of Jesus's ministry, each one is preceded by "Judas had seen Jesus . . ." Each one builds upon the other to depict the heinous nature of betrayal by one who had been closely involved with the life-giving ministry of Jesus. The musicality of this repetition is building momentum while heavily underscoring a major point that contributes to the pathos of the sermon. This repetition invites the heart response, "Judas, how *could* you!"

Haynes proceeds into his close reading of B.I.G.'s song and acknowledges that this year, 2023, marks the fiftieth anniversary of hip-hop; hence the fittingness of his sermon title and the major place given to the genre in this sermon. Hip-hop not only has influenced the content of this sermon, but it has also influenced the delivery style of the preacher. Haynes's delivery is reminiscent of the spoken word oral art form where alliteration, repetition, word play, and rhyme are major features of rhetorical and musical engagement. Haynes's version of this art form is rhythmic, metered, and driven. Sentences flow into one another without punctuation, and his hands can be seen conducting or giving definition and contour to the phrases.

Toward the end of the sermon, as it drives toward a close, Haynes's body becomes fully animated as he launches into a listing of scripture verses, each one beginning with a sequential letter of the alphabet—a feat of his unique memory. Each scripture is

---

42. Jay-Z, "Most Kingz."

Musicality and Black Preaching

prefaced by the line, "God's got your back." This has the effect of a gospel vamp, in which a phrase or line is repeated with increasing intensity while the lead singer makes intercalary commentary between repetitions. What makes this a full-blown musical moment is the addition of the organ and the heightened antiphony of the audience who are now on their feet. This is a truly orchestral, even theatrical, moment of sermonic flourish. Bodies are swaying, the preacher is stomping and jumping, the organ is riffing. Hands are clapping, and the rhythm of it all is relentless.

Once more the music pours out of the preacher as he closes, drawing on lyrics from Fanny Crosby's "At the Cross," the gospel praise song "I've Got a Feeling Everything's Gonna Be Alright," Elvina Hall's "Jesus Paid It All," and the spiritual "Glory, Glory, Hallelujah." The sermon's musical finale culminates with the preacher dancing at the pulpit, declaring, "I feel better, so much better since I laid my burdens down. And if you don't know. . . ." He points to the audience who shouts the response, "Now you know!" It is a classic mic drop ending, with the final notes conducted by the preacher and an audience finely attuned to the antiphonal musicality called for in the moment.

Music functions in a number of significant ways in this sermon. The preacher is a skilled artist, working on the palette of imagination with sound and imagery. He weaves lyrics deftly through his sermonic ideas, creating culturally appropriate resonance between thought and sound. Substantial use of anaphora underscores motifs that move in both metrical and syncopated rhythms through his sermonic material. Antiphony is both spontaneous and invited through verbal or gestural means. Phrases like "Here's your shout," or "You missed your shout right there," summon a desired response. Antiphony is crucial to the musicality of Black preaching because oral arts, such as storytelling or preaching, and musical arts, such as creating songs, have always been a communal process in Africana communities.[43] Alliteration, onomatopoeia, and similar rhetorical features create sonic patterns that reverberate throughout Haynes's delivery, serving to amplify the sermonic moves. Even the bitterness

---

43. Costen, *In Spirit and in Truth*, 9.

of betrayal is tempered in the end by the spiritual's exhortation to lay that burden down so the singer can feel better, so much better. Note how the song preaches. Note also the absence of boundary between sacred and secular in Haynes's musical choices. The lyrical fragments have the same impact; it does not matter where he draws them from. This is a demonstration of Africana indifference to such binaries—they simply do not matter. African cultures, in general, hold all of life as sacred.[44]

SINGING THAT PREACHES

The musicality of Black preaching is expressed through sermons that sing. It is also expressed through songs that preach. This chapter would not be homiletically or culturally honest if it did not offer even a brief look at this variation on the theme of preaching and music, which has been critically examined by scholars such as Braxton D. Shelley. This phenomenon of preaching songs is central to the genre of Black gospel, where artists such as Shirley Caesar and Marvin Winans count among the cadre of singing preachers who are also preaching singers. This type of preaching is of the extemporaneous, hortatory kind, marked by testimony mixed with scripture and exhortation. Caesar, who self-describes as a "singing evangelist," says about her music, "I sing a sermon and I preach a song."[45]

In her February 2022 NPR Tiny Desk concert in commemoration of Black History Month,[46] Caesar claims and demonstrates this conjoined identity. The homiletical element is clear from the start. The song's message and delivery are declarative and exhortatory, as when she punches the air with a fist, singing, "Hold on to your faith!" less than a minute into the first song. Although Caesar is seated, she accentuates her words, preacher-style, with energy and percussive movement. Not only do the singer's gestures indicate her proclamatory stance, but her intercalations also

---

44. Floyd, *Power of Black Music*, 15.
45. Caesar, *Lady, the Melody, and the Word*, Kindle loc. 520.
46. Caesar, "Shirley Caesar: Tiny Desk."

Musicality and Black Preaching

seamlessly blend the homiletical and musical. While the show's producer has billed this as a concert, the viewers have called this "a whole church service!"[47]

Elements of preaching characterize Caesar's musical delivery—hand gestures that punctuate and accentuate, scripture quotations and references to biblical narratives, a proclamatory tone in her melodic execution, and, above all, the collaborative effort between herself, her backup singers, and her musicians. No congregation sits before her, but Caesar uses the dynamics between herself and her singers to replicate that kind of reciprocal energy common in Black worship settings. Frequently in this concert the organist reiterates the pitches and syncopated rhythms of Caesar's exhortations between songs. Occasionally the organist plays a riff and Caesar repeats the musical fragment with improvisatory words. As with any dynamic aspect of Black preaching, this interplay of proclamation in word and song eludes precise description. So much of what happens is spontaneous and in response to what is sounding in the frequencies of the room at any given moment; this includes the activity of the Spirit, to which the skilled performer is attuned.

One element of gospel music that yields easily to the blend of singing and preaching is the vamp, that part toward the ending that uses repetition and ad lib to bear down on a major theme of the song's message. The function of this critical element of gospel music is closely related to the homiletical transition from climbing higher to striking fire. As Shelley explains, "Through the vamp, musical performances become interworldly events, moments when the seen world is brought into a meaningful alignment with another. In this liminal space, gospel song lyrics become something much more powerful: the living word of God."[48] In Caesar's Tiny Desk concert, there is not much room for her typically extensive use of the vamp. Yet because she cannot help but be Shirley Caesar, and because the vamp is where freedom to preach is most

---

47. One YouTube viewer's words in the comments beneath the video. Several others echoed this feedback.

48. Shelley, *Healing for the Soul*, 19.

Preaching and Music

opportune, we have a sample of it in the very introduction to this "whole church service" passing as a Tiny Desk concert.

In Caesar's first song, "It's Alright," the vamp or riff is on the word "Alright," introduced by Caesar's scream signifying the upcoming freedom to improvise. "Alright" is repeated in a four-chord structure so we hear the word sung twelve times. In the pauses between, the singer-preacher exhorts freely with admonitions such as "Don't worry about it." The vamp in a gospel song does the work of the close in a Black sermon. It opens up room for improvisation, it features the musicality of repetition, it acknowledges the presence of the Spirit. Escalation happens in volume, pace, intensity, and antiphony. Caesar's vamp signifies that this is a moment of worship; the music aims to make the presence of God felt through intoned language.

In speaking of Black preachers' love and use of language, LaRue identifies four reasons, one of which is that it "renders God present."[49] One can argue, as Turner and others do convincingly, that it is through the musicality of Black preaching that God is rendered present. Turner endorses the notion of Black preaching as krataphony—an object that opens people to an understanding of the transcendent while at the same time being rooted in the material world.[50] Rendering a transcendent God present is Caesar's aim as she tunes into that immaterial realm. At this point the singer has turned preacher, interpolating phrases of exhortation, encouragement, or warning between repeated musical phrases. The level of attunement here is high. Caesar has tapped into a divine source of energy that causes the music to rise from the mundane plane where it began. She laments the brevity of the production at one point: "I wish I had time to sing all of these songs because I'm beginning to feel something moving on the inside." Even in this closely timed, finely edited, musico-homiletical experience, the viewer can see, hear, and feel the power of preaching and music in blessed partnership.

---

49. LaRue, *I Believe I'll Testify*, 95.

50. See Turner, "Musicality of Black Preaching," in Childers and Schmit, *Performance in Preaching*, 203.

Musicality and Black Preaching

PASTOR-MUSICIAN TALKING POINTS

Because there are so many variations to this practice of musical preaching, it helps for the preacher and musician to be attuned to each other in matters of homiletical style, musical key, and genres of music. The musician typically wields more influence in Black preaching than in non-Black preaching styles and forms. One need only attend one of the major Black preaching conferences to witness this in action. The sermon's journey to celebration is a musically guided one, and in the most effective instances the entrance of musical instruments is well timed. Much of this attunement between preacher and musician happens through practice and over time, which is why some preachers will travel to guest preaching engagements with their own musicians.

For the musician, attunement means finding the tonal key in which the preacher lands once that shift in spiritual energy happens. It means being able to modulate with the preacher if she changes key. It means tuning into the flow of energy as it rises and falls throughout the sermon. It means timely entrance into the preachment rather than prematurely rushing or driving the close. It calls for the musician to be in the room for the duration of the sermon. I have heard too many preachers bemoan the practice of musicians leaving the room once the sermon has started, believing they can intuit or time when the preacher would need them. The musician's presence during the sermon enables them to listen attentively for musical hints or references to songs that may suggest a fitting musical close for the sermon. Wherever these musical references occur, the attuned musician will keep an open ear to match the spoken word with the sung word at the appropriate time. An expansive repertoire across multiple genres of music is a great asset in this relationship between the word spoken and sung. Just as enriching to a preacher's sermon preparation is their familiarity with multiple literary genres, so it is with the musician who is familiar with music across many genres, whether categorized as sacred or secular.

It is also helpful if the musician understands their primary role as proclamatory rather than performative. The proclamation of the good news is the basis of harmony between musician and preacher, without one trying to upstage the other. This was clearly demonstrated in the Caesar Tiny Desk concert, in which the musicians—keyboardist, organist, drummer, and bassist—were a team with the featured artist. The beautiful antiphonal work between preacher and musicians was a testimony to both their giftedness and spiritual attunement. When performance upstages proclamation in the musician's mind, the musician may be tempted to take the lead rather than be a team player in those moments of homiletical ecstasy. Preaching needs a partner, not a driver in those moments.

The analogy of tuning is critical to the success of the preacher-musician relationship. Early in this chapter we talked about radio frequencies. As the radio's receiver is tuned to different frequencies, it picks up different sounds being transmitted. This is a helpful concept for both musician and preacher to understand since so much of our effectiveness lies in being attuned to the Spirit of God in the room. We want to adjust our spiritual receptors to the divine frequencies. This is as critical for musician as it is for preacher. This gets both to the place where they are united in proclamation, feeding each other's creative energy, picking up divine cues because they are operating on the same wavelength. When this happens, it can truly feel magical and otherworldly. The purpose for arriving at this place of tuning is not for the emotional high it brings; rather it is toward our effectiveness in proclaiming the Word of God and manifesting the presence of God. This calls for a spirit of humility and prayer. Properly attuned, preacher and musician become human instruments played by the divine hand, sounding and voicing the word of God for the people of God.

CONCLUSION

Music is the throughline in African American worship; there is hardly an element of a church service that does not lead into or out of musical expression. Preachers and students of preaching who have been shaped by these music-infused practices come from a rich liturgical tradition, where songs preach and preaching sings. Crucial to all of this is the concept and practice of attunement, where the tuning fork of the Spirit touches our lives, sounding the key of our proclamation. In this key the harmonies of Word, preacher, song, and life together sound out the greatness and goodness of the God we proclaim.

4

Preaching and Music as Spiritual Care

THIS CHAPTER OFFERS SOME good news concerning the partnership of preaching and music in offering spiritual care. It addresses how preaching and music may be fittingly conjoined in worship as a site of God's healing grace. I once delivered a lecture to a group of seminarians titled "Preach Less, Sing More: A Faithful Pastoral Response to Congregational Stress." As a preacher and teacher of preaching, I believe in the implications of this title. There are moments in a congregation's life—and we are seeing more of these moments in recent years—when words of comfort and care need to be both heard cognitively and experienced emotively for a more fulsome expression of God's healing grace. When the preacher's response to congregational trauma depends less on speech and more on song, it can deepen the healing impact of proclamation. This chapter is a call for a more nuanced view of the sermon's role in worship as congregations deal increasingly with stressors of sickness and death, aging and shrinking membership, denominational fractures, political rancor, climate catastrophes, and violent global wars. These and other issues sometimes rise to the level of congregational trauma, where the impact is sudden, creating deep wounds with repercussions that call for psychological and spiritual remediation. Among the number of faithful and fitting responses to such trauma, the partnership of preaching and music does for proclamation what pulpit speech on its own cannot do.

Standalone preaching may be a staple in worship but, if we are honest, we will admit to its limitations in terms of what it can accomplish. A common assumption among Protestant clergy and churchgoers today is that the sermon is where the heavy lifting in worship happens. Everything else—the prayers, songs, giving, and, for some, the Communion Table—ranks as lesser in importance. There is much historical leverage beneath this assumption. The efforts of the sixteenth-century church reformers moved Protestant Christians away from the predominance of the Table to the predominance of the Word in corporate worship. Today, such congregations tend to choose pastors, not because they can balance a budget or carry a tune well, but because they can preach well. And in worship, when it comes to encountering God, or hearing God speak, a commonly shared assumption is that this happens most predictably in the sermon. Yet consider a 2017 study, done by the Pew Research Center, regarding the top reasons North Americans attend religious services. A significant majority—81 percent—of the respondents said they go to church "to become closer to God," and 66 percent of them said they go to church "for comfort in times of trouble/sorrow."[1]

WORSHIP AND HARDSHIP

The above data begs two relevant questions. First, which elements of the service facilitate congregants becoming closer to God, however that may be perceived? And second, which elements of the service offer comfort in times of trouble or sorrow? Think about

---

1. Pew Research Center, "Why Americans Go."

your own experience in worship. How would you answer these questions? While answers may vary widely, I believe that, for many of us, music is a port of entry into that meeting place of heaven and earth. Not only is there a sense of connection with God through our singing, but we also experience a sense of horizontal connection as we encounter what my Quaker friend calls "that of God" in one another through the singing. In times of congregational distress, we long to connect with God both on numinous and temporal levels. We seek to be transported into the divine realm of mystery while engaging with God among us—hearing, seeing, or touching God in one another. This multi-dimensional encounter with God is a potent source of comfort in troublesome or sorrowful times, circumstances with which we are all too familiar.

And let us just name that recent years have been hard on church folk. The years have been hard on everyone, but church folk not only have had to deal with a world of unimaginable levels of grief and loss, but they have also had to deal with shattered beliefs about sickness and death, truth and fantasy. Theodicy questions have surged like a tidal wave since the onset of our recent global pandemic. Where is God in this mess? Does God even care? Where is the storm whisperer of the Gospels? My God, why have you forsaken me? How long, oh Lord, how long?

Homiletical Insight

Pastoral responses to these questions have taken on many forms as pandemic life has gone from being a jarring anomaly to becoming a new, amorphous kind of post-pandemic normal. This shifting normality has been filled with trauma for us; it has wounded our lives, leaving its trail of disillusionment, despair, and death. It is in these times that preaching has tender work to do. Preaching does this work when it bears witness to life's hardships and when it seeks to care for the flock, tending to their anxieties and pain. These are the times in which preachers honestly name the struggles of their congregations and communities. The need for relevance invites the preacher to acknowledge the problematic lived experiences of the listeners—*and* this naming needs to come right alongside a prophetic reframing of the bad news in the redemptive light of the gospel.

This is the work of preaching to a wounded, trauma-filled congregation. It is work the biblical prophets did routinely: bifocal vision, I heard one preacher call it, through which the prophet sees the human reality right alongside the divine reality that offers hope. As preachers, we are purveyors of good news. Whatever that looks like in our given situations, it is part of the healing work of the Spirit that happens between our Good Fridays and Easter Sundays. Homiletician Kimberly Wagner uses the term "narrative fracture" to speak of the post-trauma breakdown of the narratives and theologies we use to make sense of our lives. She is focused on the preacher's response to mass traumas such as school shootings or a pandemic. The preacher's work, she says, is to offer another, more durable narrative from the perspective of God at work in the world. Wagner reminds us that "preaching that embraces narrative fracture assures individuals and communities that their experience is not beyond the presence and love of God."[2] Such assurance in worship helps draw God and people closer to one another. It is to hear this kind of blessed assurance that people often find themselves in church.

Theological Insight

Trauma-responsive worship design will see to it that worship and hardship have honest conversations. And since we're discovering all too painfully that the term "post-pandemic" only means we now have additional, lingering sources of stress and trauma, it is unreasonable to expect people to "get over it already" so we can get back to "normal worship"—another misnomer. Instead, we need to be asking ourselves as worship planners and preachers, how can our worship services speak to the levels of pain, devastation, death, and disorientation people are dealing with? Because, in the

---

2. Wagner, *Fractured Ground*, 51.

words of one Hurricane Katrina survivor, "The storm is gone, but the 'after the storm' is always here."³

This is an insight from Shelly Rambo's *Spirit and Trauma: A Theology of Remaining*. Rambo writes to help us negotiate issues of survival after traumatic events. She treats the Good Friday to Easter Sunday Triduum with pastoral sensitivity, paying special attention to the middle day—that Saturday between the two celebrated events of cross and resurrection. Rambo wants to resist "the redemptive gloss that can often be placed, harmfully, over experiences of suffering and [she wants instead] to orient us differently to the death-life narrative at the heart of the Christian tradition. Looking from the middle, we are oriented to suffering in a different way."⁴ Instead of getting over it, she urges us to figure out how to live through it, because "trauma does not go away. It persists in symptoms that live on in the body."⁵ This insight that trauma continues to live on in the body is critical information for those of us who plan and lead worship.

Psychological Insight

As worship leaders we listen up when psychologist Resmaa Menakem tells us, "The body is where we live. It's where we fear, hope, and react. It's where we constrict and relax. . . . Contrary to what many people believe, trauma is not primarily an emotional response. Trauma always happens *in the body*. It is a spontaneous protective mechanism used by the body to stop or thwart further (or future) potential damage."⁶ This has significant theological implications, which as pastors and preachers we do well to consider. When people come to worship, we may not think about meeting their physical needs. Rather, we are more inclined to think about meeting their spiritual and intellectual needs. However, our spirits,

---

3. Rambo, *Spirit and Trauma*, 2.
4. Rambo, *Spirit and Trauma*, 8.
5. Rambo, *Spirit and Trauma*, 2.
6. Menakem, *My Grandmother's Hands*, 7.

minds, hearts, souls, and bodies are intricately integrated aspects of our personhood. They are not as discrete as we often name them to be. A dip into a hot tub and yoga practice can be spiritual experiences, just as five minutes of mindful meditation can lower blood pressure and heart rate. What does all of this have to do with worship? Everything, actually.

Physiological Insight

We are commanded to love God and to worship God with all our heart, our soul, our mind, and our strength. I propose that the one time in a worship service when this is most likely to happen all at the same time is when the congregation sings. While a good sermon will engage heart and head, in many social contexts it stops short of engaging our physiological needs. Even when we recite creeds or prayers together, liturgical activities where we can potentially call upon our full selves, these activities do not place significant demand upon the body. But when it is time to sing, at least five of our bodily systems are engaged: the circulatory, muscular, nervous, cardiovascular, and respiratory systems all come into play. The tongue, teeth, lips, and hard and soft palates come into play. The vocal cords vibrate and send sound into the sinus and chest cavities. Lungs, diaphragm, and a plethora of muscles spring into action as our bodies engage in the act of singing. And if we are standing and the song has a compelling rhythm, other muscle groups get in on the action as we might sway, clap, or dance. Our breathing becomes synchronized as we inhale and exhale from phrase to phrase, line to line. Trauma experts tell us that "reconnecting people to their own breath is an essential first step in trauma healing.... For those who experience trauma, regaining access to one's own breath is a gateway to reconnection."[7] And all of this is at an individual level. Imagine what happens to a group of people doing this all at the same time.

---

7. Rambo, *Spirit and Trauma*, 163.

Preaching and Music

Musical Insight

Group singing is highly recommended by therapists and other psychological practitioners. In his book, Menakem laments, "Unfortunately much of what Americans say and do is designed to keep our bodies out of harmony with each other. Our public discourse, our media, and our policing all unsettle our bodies far more than they help us settle them."[8] On the other hand, we can help each other heal when our bodies come into harmony with one another. What is happening when we inhale that preparatory breath before we sing the first note of the song? What is happening when we sing in the same key, the same words, at the same pace, with the same rhythms, and even occasionally harmonize pitches into soprano, alto, tenor, and bass parts? Our bodies vibrate sympathetically as the air waves around us shimmer to produce tonalities where sometimes it sounds like a meeting of heaven and earth. Some would say this is holy ground. Others would say this is not only holy but healing ground. Congregational singing, therefore, is a path to individual and congregational health as our bodies are put to work, often subconsciously dislodging embedded trauma through somatic or physical activity. The more congregations sing, the more they are disposed to good health and healing. Healing of our bodies, our minds, our hearts, our souls, our very lives can happen as we sing together.

Insight from the Pew

Some would say singing together does healing work in their relationships. Poet and lyricist Lindy Thomson gives voice to this idea in a blog post created before the outbreak of COVID-19 made singing together dangerous. Based on the sheer number of her readers who asked permission to reprint her blog post, dated January 4, 2019, she clearly speaks for many of us when she writes:

---

8. Menakem, *My Grandmother's Hands*, 181.

Preaching and Music as Spiritual Care

I might be exhausted and the children might be cranky,
but I will be going to church on Sunday.
Don't know who is preaching, doesn't matter—
the sermon may be helpful or not, holds my attention or doesn't—
it's the singing.
I go to sing.
I get up,
get clean,
get dressed,
possibly get mad (at not-ready kids, at empty coffee pot, at traffic)
get going,
get there,
get seated,
get comfortable,
get focused
and when the music starts,
get saved.
It's the singing.
I go to sing.

It's the willingness to *stand if you are able*,
the common agreement on page number,
the voluntary sharing of songbooks with people on your row,
even ones you rode there with—
but most of all,
it's the collective in-breath before the first sound is made,
the collective drawing upon the grace of God,
the collective, if inadvertent, admission
that we are all human,
all fragile,
all in need of the sustaining air, freely dispensed,
all in need of each other to get the key right and not sound discordant—
it's the hidden life-celebration
in the act of making a joyful noise,
all together.
We don't even have to sound that good.
Singing together still brings home
the we-ness of worship,
the *not-alone*-ness of life in God,
the best of all we have to offer each other.

> When we are singing, I think that I might actually be able to forgive you
> for being so terribly human,
> and you might be able to forgive me
> for being so terribly not there yet,
> and we might be able to find peace *now*,
> not postpone it for some heavenly hereafter
> but live and breathe it today,
> drawing in the grace of God,
> voicing out our need and hope and gratitude and longing.
> When we are singing, I can feel the better world coming,
> and if I get to be a part of it, you do too . . .
>
> so sing with me,
> and we'll make our way down that blessed road together,
> collectively better
> than we ever thought
> possible.[9]

Thompson recalls that the piece received decent feedback when she originally posted it in January 2019. Fast-forward another eighteen to twenty months and, in her words, "It mysteriously revived itself and was suddenly everywhere, with no initiating action on my part. I think the pandemic made people see the poem in a different light. It really hit a nerve."[10] It is an easy guess that the collective nerve struck was the forced silencing of voices joined together in song, voices deprived of that sense of the "we-ness of worship and the not-alone-ness of life in God." This period of not-singing-together was exacerbated by the harm done in virtual worship that left preaching standing on its own liturgically to do the overwhelming work of pastoral care. There was no more collective inhale—"drawing in the grace of God"—and exhale—"voicing out our need"—afforded by communal activity that could work to dislodge some of the trauma retained in our bodies. That grace

---

9. Thompson, "I Go to Sing." Used with author's permission.
10. Email conversation with the author, August 27, 2023.

of God, that healing grace, permeates Thompson's reflections on this poem years later, as she reminds us, "Grace is in the singing."[11]

LITURGICAL APPROACHES TO SPIRITUAL CARE

Up to this point we have looked at historical, homiletical, theological, psychological, physiological, musical, and congregational perspectives of preaching and music. These have shown us the need for, and impact of, trauma-responsive preaching and congregational singing. We now turn to more pragmatic matters. What are some ways in which preaching and music might be conjoined in worship as a site of healing grace? What historical or contemporary models can tutor us as we tend to wounded souls?

Use of Hymn Lyrics and Sermon Framing

In chapter 2 we looked at the benefits of framing the sermon with songs that share what the sermon says and what it hopes to do. The preacher may pull into the body of the sermon fragments of those lyrics used to frame the sermon or lyrics used earlier in the service. The poetry, with its images and metaphors, adds rhetorical texture to the sermon and can make it more accessible to hurting hearts. If the preacher has the voice or courage for it, they may sing that fragment or two, gesturing for the congregation to join in. I have found it helpful at the start of the sermon to alert listeners that songs will surface throughout the preaching. I have let them know they are welcome to hum or sing along should I break out into song. A trauma-informed preacher can take this approach knowing that the bodily work of singing affords healing of the soul, that trauma retentions can be released as people sing or hum together.[12] If the preacher does not have a singing voice or the nerve to break into song, it is helpful to remember that hymns or songs of comfort and healing do not always need to be sung to do their

---

11. Thompson, "I Do, in Fact, Go to Sing," 35.
12. Menakem, *My Grandmother's Hands*, 191.

therapeutic work. Lyrics of such songs, especially if familiar, will conjure the music at the sound of the words. Simply quoting, "and God will raise you up on eagle's wings, bear you on the breath of dawn, make you to shine like the sun, and hold you in the palm of God's hand"[13] will bring the comforting melody into the room, especially if the spoken words mirror the lyrical cadence of the sung words.

Reference to Backstories

Many songs of comfort were written by authors going through or reflecting on their own personal discomfort. When used as sermon illustrations or examples, the backstories to such songs can partner with the sermon and the song in proclaiming peace to stormy souls. One compiler of hymn stories begins the entry for "What a Friend We Have in Jesus" with the question, "How does a personal poem written to a mother from a despondent son, recently immigrated from England to a relatively remote section of Canada in the mid-nineteenth century, become one of the most widely sung hymns in the world?"[14] Indeed, the biography of this hymn's author is filled with enough personal tragedy to qualify him as being in touch with the individual and collective sorrow in the room. Uniting the traumatic experiences of songwriters with the existential sorrow of the singers is an act of compassion on the preacher's part. I offer one word of caution here: it is worthwhile to compare a few sources to corroborate the facts, as there are many spurious, unsubstantiated stories available regarding hymn origins and compositions. I recommend, among other fine sources, *The Canterbury Dictionary of Hymnology*, Discipleship Ministries History of Hymns online, the website Hymnary.org, and the online Cyberhymnal. The Calvin Institute of Christian Worship website contains several informative articles, including one by Joan Huyser-Honig that includes a number of useful hyperlinks,

---

13. Joncas, "On Eagle's Wings," 143.
14. Hawn, "History of Hymns: What a Friend."

titled "Sharing Hymn Stories Invites Worshipers into Experience." Searching a library catalog with the keywords "hymn stories" will also yield helpful published resources.

Musical Transitions

The preacher may be using a sermonic form that has moments of shifting from one perspective to another, from problem to resolution or from despair to hope. When music is incorporated into the sermon, it can facilitate these moments of transition, creating a moment for reflection and some cognitive breathing space. Breathing space allows important ideas to marinate or sink in; it is as important to a sermon as rests are to music. A musical transition may link different movements within a memorial service or prayer vigil—see the example in the special services section later. It may also be a moment within the sermon, as in Tom Troeger's sermon on Balm in Gilead, also discussed later in the chapter.

I vividly recall an effective use of this technique in a sermon on gratitude.[15] It provided spiritual care, not in an acute situation, but in a seemingly preemptive way. The preacher used the nonliturgical earworm "Thank You for Hearing Me," by the late Sinéad O'Connor, as a sung transition in between five sermonic moves. This refrain functioned much like the sung response in the reading of a psalm in that it allowed the congregation to participate at intervals by repeatedly casting a musical spotlight on the focal point of the spoken word. During Rev. Brown's sermon, the song was led *a capella* each time by the worship pastor, who was seated in the chancel area, symbolically sharing the preaching space. With each repetition of the song the original gerund, "hearing," was replaced by another, such as loving, seeing, or creating. On occasion the syntax of the phrase was reworked: "and for forgiving me," or "thanks for amazing me." When my preaching class viewed this YouTube recording, they were grateful to have watched and listened to this rather than reading the manuscript; watching gave

---

15. Brown, "Power of Giving."

them an immersive experience in which they could simulate what the impact might have been on the congregation present. I asked them to sing along with the words on the screen. Their feedback included observations such as "the song tied together what would otherwise have seemed like disparate parts of the sermon," and "by the end it was the song really doing the preaching." The idea of using a song with the words "thank you" or "thanks for" gave potency to this sermon that was meant to motivate the congregation to find ways of expressing gratitude throughout the week. A song fragment or refrain positioned transitionally within a sermon assists the preacher and the Spirit to proclaim through sensory and embodied means. And if it is an earworm, like O'Connor's song, may it be ever so thoughtfully chosen!

Lamenting with the Psalmists

The biblical psalms offer us meaningful ways to partner preaching with music in times of trauma, trouble, and sorrow. The psalmists granted equal opportunity to praise and complain in their song lyrics. Granted, some of these songs may well make us wonder how they found their place in the Hebrew "hymnal," with their vengeful, imprecatory language.[16] Yet these songs, much like the African American spirituals, were created against the backdrop of a God who was always there, always listening, and always able to make a difference, in spite of how the poet was feeling in that moment of the psalm's creation. This background or backdrop of faith in a living, powerful God, the God of their ancestry, enabled the psalmists to give thanks and complain with the same vigor. Their lament was authentic, and it was necessary to help them address the trauma and process the pain of their existence. The psalms and psalmists teach us how to use the artistry of poetry and song as ways to give voice to distressing thoughts and disturbing feelings. Nothing is off limits in our lament; from personal betrayal to national catastrophes, the psalms model honest grief expressed in

---

16. Borger, Tel, and Witvliet, *Psalms for All Seasons*, v–vi.

Preaching and Music as Spiritual Care

worship. Scripture indexes at the back of hymnals or a search for the psalm's verses in an online search field may produce options for singing and preaching on the same psalm.

Special Services

In the life of every congregation there are special services that help to ritualize loss, process grief, and honor memory. Funerals and memorial services, prayer vigils, All Saints, and Blue Christmas or Longest Night services are among the most common. The degree of effectiveness of these services correlates to the degree with which music is incorporated in offering care and proclaiming good news. In *Accompany Them with Singing: The Christian Funeral*, Tom Long advocates for copious amounts of congregational singing "to be heard above the noisy clamor of death."[17]

In the All Saints' Day sermon at the end of this chapter, I watched people become visibly moved as they helped me conclude the sermon by singing the final verses of "What Wondrous Love Is This?"[18] The feedback from that sermon was copious. It bore evidence that the singing performed healing work for persons there who were grieving painful losses of that year or years before. One flushed, tearful congregant said to me, "Thank you for the singing. It was so . . . cathartic." She had paused, mentally searching for the word, before cathartic came emphatically to her lips. I interpreted her look of combined puzzlement and relief to mean that for her this catharsis was as unexpected as it was needed. We do not know how this healing happens with musical proclamation; neither can we orchestrate it, since much depends on the experience and perspective of the individuals involved. Suffice it to say there is a potential in this sermon-song dyad that preachers can tap into for the sake of spiritual care and soul tending in times when souls are tender. The pianist for the service that day had recently lost her husband to death. She played the postlude for the service through

---

17. Long, *Accompany Them with Singing*, 172.
18. Anon., "What Wondrous Love Is This?"

Preaching and Music

tears, her fingers moving deftly and soulfully across the keys in a jazz arrangement of "When the Saints Go Marching In" that perfectly capped the service. Proclaimed on the keys by someone experiencing hardship, it was a deeply inspiring and uplifting message with which to end a weighty worship gathering.

A second experience of this powerful partnership of preaching and music was an even more difficult service I attended: a vigil held on the evening of the day a twelve-year-old girl had been found brutally murdered. This was a congregation in the grip of a violent crisis. There was no time for careful planning, but a care-filled gathering was necessary. The worship director, three of the church's retired pastors, and I landed on a service of Word, prayer, and song. Four movements organized the service, each one featuring a passage of scripture, a brief meditation by a minister, a congregational song, and a prayer. No one element lasted any longer than five minutes; this created constant motion within the consistency of a pattern. People could move their bodies by singing, standing during the songs, approaching the altar rail to stand or kneel, or going to one of three candle-lighting stations in the room. Preaching was informal, a reflection on the scripture that had been read, and it was brief.

The singing was heartfelt. Songs such as "I Want Jesus to Walk with Me," "Stand by Me," "What a Friend We Have in Jesus," and "Through It All" were part of this congregation's canon of heart songs. This United Methodist congregation needed "strength in tribulation," the subtitle of the section of their hymnal from which the songs for that evening were taken. The grief in the room was raw. Bodies were agitated. Minds were numb. Tears flowed freely as the music, interspersed with sermonic reflections, opened space for the palpable grief in the room to be expressed without judgment. Singing gave the people "something to do" in these moments, as did lighting the candles and reading aloud together familiar passages like the Twenty-Third Psalm. As they dispersed, some people reported feeling better, some felt less devastated, and for others the service had tempered their rage over the tragedy. Someone said the hour spent in communal mourning felt like a heart massage. People who did not or could not sing received the therapeutic benefit nonetheless as waves of sound made by surrounding human bodies washed over them. In those emotionally fragile moments preaching and music did together what neither had the capacity to do on its own.

Use of Healing Hymns That Preach

Hymn writers have given us several excellent songs written on related scripture passages of healing that can be used to proclaim in tandem. Upon close reading we find some of them do due diligence to "interpret scripture in poetically beautiful, easily accessible, and pastorally empowering ways."[19] In a pastoral care sermon, the preacher may expound on both the hymn and its companion biblical text. One such example is J. Dudley Weaver's "The Woman Hiding in the Crowd."[20] The first three stanzas paraphrase the encounter between Jesus and the woman with the issue of blood as recorded in Mark's and Luke's Gospels. The hymn's final two verses put the congregation in the woman's place: "The burdens now that weigh us down, the sins we fear to speak, the ache of heart and empty soul we lay before your feet. So touch us, Lord, with healing grace and make us whole again that we may always live in you and know your peace within."[21] This hymn has five verses, the first three of which are descriptive. For homiletical effectiveness these first three can be sung before or during the first part of the sermon. The final two that mark the turn toward the good news may be sung anywhere near the end with therapeutic effect.

Another contemporary hymn that proclaims healing is Tom Troeger's "Silence! Frenzied, Unclean Spirit." The editorial note in one hymnal reads, "Based on Mark 1:21–28/Luke 4:31–37, this text recalls how Jesus exorcized a demon, ponders what demons mean today, and concludes with a prayer for wholeness. It is set here to

---

19. Troeger, *Wonder Reborn*, 30.
20. Weaver, "Woman Hiding in the Crowd."
21. Weaver, "Woman Hiding in the Crowd," 178.

a familiar Welsh tune whose recurring three-note figures help to convey a sense of internal turmoil."[22] Troeger wrote this hymn out of his encounters as a pastor with people experiencing "profound emotional turmoil." He says, "I wanted to draw on the strength of Christ's exorcism for facing these painful situations."[23] Indeed, the lyrics of this hymn will find strong resonance with many suffering from mental health diagnoses. Many congregations take advantage of Mental Health Awareness Month to raise congregational sensitivity around health matters that are too often erased by silence in our worship. The third verse of Troeger's hymn frames a tender plea: "Silence, Christ, the unclean spirit in our mind and in our heart. Speak your word that when we hear it all our demons shall depart. Clear our thought and calm our feeling, still the fractured, warring soul. By the power of your healing make us faithful, true, and whole."[24] This hymn's metrical pattern makes it singable to more than one tune, but the tune AUTHORITY is probably the most compatible with the disturbing aspects of mental disease.

Other hymns that may be used as sermonic material include "We Have the Strength to Lift and Bear,"[25] based on the Markan narrative of the four friends who carried the paralytic man to Jesus; "We Yearn, O Christ for Wholeness,"[26] a hymn inspired by a sermon on disability; and "When We Must Bear Persistent Pain," inspired by the author's own experience of debilitating migraine headaches.[27] Hymns, with their strophic patterns that lend themselves to extended reflection and storytelling, do credible sermonic work. Here is an example of a compelling sermon based on a hymn written not on a single text, but on the theme of dementia, a ubiquitous disability with which aging congregations are all too familiar.

22. Troeger, "Silence!" in *Glory to God*, 181, footnote to hymn.
23. Troeger, "Silence!" in *New Century Hymnal*, 176, footnote to hymn.
24. Troeger, "Silence!"
25. Troeger, "We Have the Strength," 178.
26. Carlson, "We Yearn," 179.
27. Duck, "When We Must Bear Persistent Pain," 807.

Preaching and Music as Spiritual Care

EXAMPLE 1—"LOVE LINGERING"

Mary Louise Bringle's hymn "When Memory Fades" was the text around which the preacher built this All Saints' Day sermon, "Love Lingering."[28] The preacher, Rev. Jane Dutton, the congregation's associate pastor for congregational care and connection, leaned into her role; she offered care and facilitated vital connections on this day of sober reflection on human mortality.

When Memory Fades

When memory fades and recognition falters,
when eyes we love grow dim, and minds confused,
speak to our souls of love that never alters;
speak to our hearts by pain and fear abused.
O God of life and healing peace, empower us
with patient courage, by your grace infused.

As frailness grows, and youthful strengths diminish
in weary arms, which worked their earnest fill.
your aging servants labor now to finish
their earthly tasks, as fits your mystery's will.
We grieve their waning, yet rejoice, believing
your arms, unwearied, shall uphold us still.

Within your spirit, goodness lives unfading.
The past and future mingle into one.
All joys remain, un-shadowed light pervading.
No valued deed will ever be undone.
Your mind enfolds all finite acts and offerings.
Held in your heart, our deathless life is won![29]

"Love Lingers" was three years in the making as Dutton, the senior pastor, and the music minister discussed how best to incorporate the Bringle hymn and the theme of dementia into this annual service, when grief and loss are at the forefront of many people's minds. Sometimes it is easier to work through a difficult sermonic topic when we can sing about it. The sermon form is what Christine

---

28. Dutton, "Love Lingering."
29. Bringle, "When Memory Fades," 808. Used with permission.

Smith would call a woven sermon,[30] a result of the preacher's interweaving meaningful fragments of the hymn's lyrics with stories and eyewitness accounts of giving care to aging and dying members of the congregation and her family. These stories, organized around the hymn, create connections with home-bound members. They bring to life the theology of a community of saints—absent yet made present that morning through accounts of their lives. The lingering love of God expressed through human love and care is the focus of the sermon. As to its function, the preacher hopes those listening would both be comforted by this love and use it as a lens through which to view the losses that accompany aging.

The sermon is a series of moves, each tied to some part of the hymn. The hymn is not only the organizing factor but a thread that seams the sermon's disparate parts. The overwhelming response of listeners, after the fact, bore witness to the effectiveness of this conjoining of sermon and song. Listeners' responses included words like "touching and thoughtful," "nurturing and binding broken places," "warmed my heart," and "a source of wisdom about the divine." One listener who knew the hymn's author shared the link of the service with Dr. Bringle, who responded, "I was so moved by the elegant and eloquent sermon that your colleague drew from the text to 'When Memory Fades.'"[31] This practice of preaching on a hymn text is time-tested. I encourage students and practitioners to do close readings of the congregation's favorites for possible texts that can preach, particularly on special occasions. I also encourage them to become familiar with the newer hymns being written by living composers. Many of these are gems of biblical interpretation and thematic reflection.

EXAMPLE 2—BALM IN GILEAD

Shorter, cyclical, non-strophic songs are also capable of preaching care and healing; the genre of African American spirituals does this homiletical work well. The spiritual "Balm in Gilead" is the

30. Smith, *Weaving the Sermon*, 8.
31. Email from Rev. Dutton to author, November 24, 2022.

primary text for Tom Troeger's sermon, printed in its entirety in his chapter appropriately titled "To Make the Wounded Whole."[32] Troeger's sermonic delivery incorporates instrumental, vocal, solo, and congregational iterations of the spiritual. "Balm in Gilead" is an interpretative response by enslaved African Americans to the series of questions in Jeremiah 8:22, "Is there no balm in Gilead? Is there no physician there? Why then has the health of my poor people not been restored?" In preaching on the spiritual and the Jeremiah text in tandem, Troeger's close reading of each does solid, interpretive work. He compares the "religious violence and spiritual" hunger of both communities—the ancient community in which Jeremiah was embedded and the enslaved community out of which the spiritual emerged. Troeger's exegetical work of both social contexts is well-resourced by scholars of the Hebrew Bible and African American history. The sermon wraps itself around the prophet's questions. The preacher confronts the issues of violence done in the name of religion and the accompanying hunger for spiritual remediation.

With pastoral sensitivity the preacher visits the answer found in the ancient balm:

> There are three things to note about a balm. First, it is not a single pure substance but a mixture of resin and oils. Second, a balm is not an elixir, it is not a miracle drug, it is not a quick cure, it is not an instant fix. Upon application a balm is soothing. It brings some relief, but it does not erase the wound overnight. A balm does not relieve sorrow all at once. Third, the balm nurtures the process of healing, but that process is a function of something greater than the balm alone. The restoration of skin and flesh comes from the body itself, from its own energies for wholeness and heath.[33]

The preacher uses these three aspects of the balm—as central to the scripture as they are to the spiritual—to illuminate the powerful, enduring quality of the spirituals and the work they did in the enslaved community that turned Jeremiah's question into an

32. Troeger, *Wonder Reborn*, 41–48.
33. Troeger, *Wonder Reborn*, 44.

affirmation.[34] At a transitional sermonic moment the preacher pauses for an instrumental rendition of the spiritual that gives people time to reflect on what they have just heard. This is a pivotal point in the sermon where music assists the preacher to proclaim by creating space for reflection, that cognitive breathing space referred to earlier in this chapter.

When he resumes speaking, Troeger turns the listeners' attention to themselves, living in their own Gilead. He ultimately calls the church to be the balm for wounds inflicted upon our society.

> In an age of religious violence and spiritual hunger, the church is a balm whenever it truly becomes a religious/spiritual community. Remember: a balm is not an elixir, not a quick fix, not a miracle drug. But over time, a balm brings healing. It sets off a process of thought and action, of prayer and art, of belief and practice, of conversation and community. Over time it will bring healing and wholeness to a world of religious violence and spiritual hunger. Yes, there is a balm in Gilead to make the wounded whole.[35]

Following this poignant invitational ending, the congregation sings the spiritual.

The impact of this conjoining of sermon and song is the hermeneutical resonance between scripture text and hymn text. It gives deeper relevance to Jeremiah's questions while simultaneously enriching the homiletical and pastoral value of the hymn. Blending sermon and song also enables continued proclamation of Troeger's message after the service is over. The exegesis so closely harmonizes sermon, scripture, and song, that people singing this song or humming its melody on their way home are more likely to recall the sermon's function—to enable them to see the church as a balm for society's wounds—even as the song serves as a balm for their own wounds. Sermon and song can together offer soul care so much more effectively than either can on its own. The spirituals tended to the souls of their composing communities then even as they do for their singing communities now.

34. Thurman, *Deep River*, 57.
35. Troeger, *Wonder Reborn*, 48.

Preaching and Music as Spiritual Care

HOW THE SPIRITUALS TEACH US

Like many psalms the spirituals proclaim the good news right alongside the bad news; they give equal opportunity to both despair and hope. The spirituals provide for preachers not just a resource for sermonic work, but a sturdy homiletical model that views "death as a necessary climate for hope."[36] These spiritual sermons emerged organically from the lives of a people for whom hope and comfort were no cheap spiritual commodities flowing from the lips of a practiced, polished pulpiteer. Rather, their hope and comfort grew defiantly out of the blood-soaked soil of their daily lives. Powery notes that "the term hope is rarely, if ever, used in a spiritual, revealing that hope is not generated by articulating the word. Hope in spiritual preaching bubbles up when death is not fixated upon and viewed as the whole gospel story."[37] The whole gospel story includes both Good Friday and Easter Sunday. Just as there is no joy of resurrection apart from the devastation of crucifixion, preachers do well to let the spirituals assist us to proclaim this juxtaposition of death and hope.[38]

The spirituals show us how to keep measured pace in the movement from lament to hope. In her counsel to preachers Kimberly Wagner remarks that "lament has the capacity to ground and support those who find themselves disoriented and fragmented due to trauma, while also helping the community to find voice and agency to respond in sustainable ways."[39] Disoriented and fragmented are accurate albeit understated descriptors of the African peoples bought and sold in colonized North America. Their world had been shattered, yet somehow, they were able to find value in the shards that contained important cultural memories, such as singing together. It was more than singing together; their singing was also praying, crying, dancing, storytelling (preaching), and creating on

---

36. Powery, *Dem Dry Bones*, 59.
37. Powery, *Dem Dry Bones*, 59.
38. See Powery's guide for authentic juxtaposition of death and hope in *Dem Dry Bones*, 57–69.
39. Wagner, *Fractured Ground*, 8.

the fly through their well-honed improvisatory gifts. Singing was how they interpreted and responded to a life filled with hardship.

Spirituals can help us understand hope in more nuanced ways. Taking our cue from Powery, we can let the spirituals teach us how to let music be our companion and guide in the midst of hardship. They can teach us to take things slow in the movement from despair to hope and from problem to solution, and to take seriously the climate of death in which hope is nurtured.[40] The spirituals often proclaim death as the hope: "When the enslaved sang, 'and before I'd be a slave, I'd be buried in my grave and go home to my Lord and be free,' this equated death with freedom."[41] This view of death may be especially poignant in grieving the loss of a person who died after a tumultuous or seemingly interminable struggle with illness or disease; release from the body sometimes means relief and longed-for peace.

The spirituals also teach us economy of language in the face of loss. As I instruct my preaching students when preparing funeral sermons, words are not always the best treatment for the kinds of emotions grieving people are dealing with. The preacher may be making wise, comforting pronouncements, but their proliferation of words can begin to sound like meaningless babble to heavy, grief-laden hearts. The economy of words and dependence upon imagery is a lesson from the spirituals for the preacher who strives to be trauma responsive. "Swing low, sweet chariot, coming for to carry me home"[42] bears a poignant image sturdy enough to hold a grief-laden heart. The simplicity of "dark midnight was my cry, give me Jesus"[43] with its plaintive tune needs little, if any, explanation. And the image of stealing away to Jesus as "the trumpet sounds within my soul"[44] brings a deep comfort that is hard to match with any of our churchy platitudes around death.

---

40. Powery, *Dem Dry Bones*, 59–60.
41. Powery, *Dem Dry Bones*, 61.
42. "Swing Low, Sweet Chariot," Traditional, African American Spiritual.
43. "Give Me Jesus," Traditional, African American Spiritual.
44. "Steal Away," Traditional, African American Spiritual.

Preaching and Music as Spiritual Care

The preacher, willing to call upon the healing graces of congregational song to make the wounded whole, has a trove of resources at their disposal. They will find their pastoral burden lighter, shared by the community of saints ministering in song to one another in all the aspects that make up our personhood, including body, soul, and spirit. Through carefully selected music our sermons will be re-preached as songs associated with our sermons come to mind long after the preaching is over.

PASTOR-MUSICIAN TALKING POINTS

I offer a few questions intended to prompt the kinds of conversations pastors and music ministers need to have around this partnership of preaching and music in response to congregational distress. What are our congregation's heart songs—the songs likely to surface from their hearts in times of trouble and sorrow? How can we vet or screen these songs for their theological and musical value, knowing that we are on congregational "holy ground" here? What might be the thematic gaps in this collection of well-known music that offers congregational care, and how can we go about filling those gaps? At the actual service, what determines the tenor of the liturgy and how might we collaborate to bring that about?

It is a beautiful thing when both pastor and music minister have an active, working knowledge of the congregation's canon of favorites from a theological and musical perspective. I say beautiful because it demonstrates deep knowledge and understanding of the flock they are both caring for. In the absence of such knowledge, it helps to figure out together how to curate such a list, whether by poll, survey, year-long tracking, or some other means. Times of crisis call for us to have an occasion-specific reservoir of resources from which we can draw. Since these occasions give us little to no time to prepare or do the research, an active, working knowledge of the congregation's heart songs should be in the toolkits of both preacher and musician.

The question then follows, how can we screen this collection theologically and musically? The musical perspective is crucial.

Preaching and Music

When alternative tunes are available, some may be better suited for certain occasions than others. Some may be better suited for aging voices than for younger singers. Blessed is the team that finds many musically healthy songs with which to work. Theological scrutiny is also critical. Do these songs proclaim in alignment with what the singing community believes to be true about God, about themselves, and about God's world? What do these songs teach about sickness, grief, loss, and death?

Once this list has been musically and theologically vetted, then begins the task of discovering what gaps may need to be filled. Congregational favorites are favored for their sentimental value, often some association with the song that generates nostalgic memories or feelings of comfort. It helps worship leaders to remember that "memories, values, and beliefs attach to particular texts and tunes, which, on being sung, embody our faith and support our daily life as Christians."[45] Missing from this repertoire of favorites may be songs that challenge, lament, or teach about current situations such as homelessness or disability justice; these gaps tend to be congregation specific. Pastor and musician together can embark on a plan to enrich the congregation's playlist. The added songs may not become favorites, but they can at least become familiar.

This leads to the question, where can we find new music that assists the preacher(s) to proclaim the whole gospel? For churches that use a hymnal, the answer may be in the pew pockets or on the pastor's or musician's bookshelf. For those who do not, I refer you to the online resources recommended in the appendix. However this question is answered, it needs to be followed up with a workable, year-round plan for teaching this new music. See my recommendations in chapter 2 for ways to expand the congregation's repertoire. This expansion works best when these new texts are woven into the sermon or used as an organizing principle for crafting the sermon. When we find a hymn that will preach, it is a precious gift to the community of Christ.

Sometimes the music that offers spiritual care may be dealing with a painful topic about which people can sing their way to a place

---

45. Duck, *Worship for the Whole People*, 87.

of ease. The hymn-writer Carolyn Winfrey Gillette has skillfully incorporated a number of trauma-inducing situations into musical prayers and proclamations. The topical index of her website lists hymns that address such concerns as abuse by clergy, aging, disabilities and abilities, gun violence, homelessness, natural disasters, pandemic, terrorism, and violence.[46] Reviewing this new material together can open pastor and musician to exciting possibilities as Gillette's trademark is her use of familiar hymn tunes for new lyrics.

Finally, what determines the affective character of the service, and how do we together create this? Often the situation generating the service will create its own tone. The way a person died, the personality of the deceased or their dying wishes, the impact of the situation on the congregation, or the cultural inclinations of the gathered group—all require levels of listening and being attuned to the situation. Collaboration is critical in these moments of deciding the tenor of the moment; it ensures the perspective is not one-dimensional. The tenor of the service can be created in several ways: visually, vocally, through choice of liturgical material, and especially through the music selected. Some congregations or denominational traditions are more disposed to celebration at funerals and memorial services while others care more for somber reflection. Once the nature of the service is determined it is the wise pastor and musician who will examine both text and tune for compatibility with each other and with the character of the service. The pastor would do well to lean on the musician's training and experience in this regard; musical sensibilities will pay attention to tune, tempo, and instrumentation to achieve the desired outcome. This conversation will be most productive when both ministers share the assumption that music is doing its fair share in proclaiming and providing Christ's comfort and strength.

Congregational stress and communal trauma are all too real in the living of these days. Yet the merger of preaching and music in response to these demands can offer people who attend our services a way to become closer to God, to find comfort in times of

---

46. Gillette, "Hymns by Carolyn Winfrey Gillette."

trouble and sorrow. May our proclamation of God's goodness and mercy bring pulpit and pew together in resonant grace.

SAMPLE SERMON—"FROM HARDSHIP TO WORSHIP"

The lectionary text Revelation 7:9–17 formed the biblical foundation for this All Saints' Day sermon preached in a chapel service at Lancaster Theological Seminary. In the audience were students, faculty, and staff, including the seminary chaplain. In this sermon, "From Hardship to Worship," Revelation's saints invite and inspire us into singing as a means of grace.

∼

Good morning, friends of God. Two things—First, this sermon sits squarely in the context of All Saints' Day. For some this is a day of comfort, for others it is a day of pain. If you find yourself in a place of discomfort, I encourage you to tend to your need, in whatever way is best for you. Our chaplain is here for your support if needed. Second, in the course of preaching, if I break out into singing and you know the song, by all means feel free to join me!

And so we pray.... (Chalice Hymnal #22)

> Lord Jesus Christ, be present now
> Our hearts in true devotion bow
> Thy Spirit send with grace divine
> And let thy truth within us shine
> Unseal our lips to sing (speak) thy praise
> Our souls to thee in worship raise
> Make strong our faith, increase our light
> That we may know thy name aright
> Till we with saints in glad accord
> Sing holy, holy is the Lord
> And in the light of heaven above
> Shall see thy face and know thy love.[47]

---

47. Wilhelm, "Lord Jesus Christ be Present Now," 524.

Today, we pray these things in the name of the slaughtered Lamb, Jesus the Christ. Amen.

"Mom, I have good news and bad news, which one do you want first?" When my daughter begins a conversation like this, my response is the same: "Give me the bad news first." Well, here I am this morning, a minister of the good news of Jesus Christ, but I also have bad news. And I am going to give it to you in my preferred order—bad news first. Life is hard! Life is messed up! And is it just me or is it getting harder and more messed up by the day? We wake up each morning dreading the news that might greet us—it doesn't matter which news network we watch because news networks make their profits by publishing bad news.

So we hear heart-wrenching reports about the unspeakable horrors of over 110 armed conflicts currently happening in Latin America, Europe, Asia, Africa, and the Middle East.[48] We hear of lives being upended by famines and natural disasters, of millions of people being forced to leave their homes in search of asylum or shelter. On the national scene we are saddened and angered by political and ideological shenanigans eroding our confidence in our highest-paid public servants. We hear terrifying news, almost daily it seems lately, of mass shootings, each one deepening our state of shock or outrage or numbness. Then there's death—opioid-related, suicide-related, COVID-related, gun-related death—that Just. Won't. Stop! And I haven't even named our personal troubles yet. Life is hard. And on this day Christians commemorate as All Saints' Day, one particular hardship is front and center—death, with its companions, grief and loss.

This is the context of our scripture text today in verses 9 through 17 of Revelation chapter 7. Revelation is written to first-century Christ-followers encountering death, grief, and loss, while fearing for their lives. The letter-writer is John, who self-describes as "your brother who shares with you in Jesus the persecution and the kingdom and the patient endurance" (Revelation 1:9). If you've read Revelation, you know it does not shy away from

---

48. Geneva Academy of International Humanitarian Law and Human Rights, "Today's Armed Conflicts."

Preaching and Music

violence, death, or hardship. That's precisely because it was written to Christians whose daily living involved the hardship of often violent persecution for their faith. Many of them were martyred—tortured, thrown into arenas with wild beasts, boiled in oil, burned alive—all for confessing Jesus rather than Caesar as Lord. And as John writes to encourage them to remain faithful, he invites them into his apocalyptic vision of a world where wrongs are made right, diabolical rulers get their due, and the true and living God emerges ultimately as King of kings and Lord of lords.

In this vision, with its startling and often bizarre scenes of cosmic conflict, there is something that keeps happening regularly and often randomly. People and heavenly beings break out into singing! As out of place as it may seem to have songs juxtaposed with conflict and death, this is one hallmark of Revelation, where at least "fifteen hymns or hymn-fragments are commonly recognized."[49] Some scholars would argue for more. The four living creatures are singing, the elders are singing, angels are singing, every living creature in heaven and earth is singing, an innumerable multitude from every nation, tribe, people, and language is singing, unidentified loud voices are singing, warriors are singing, even an inanimate altar is personified as singing! Some of this singing or liturgical chanting is so loud the decibel levels are equivalent to the roar of rushing waters (think Niagara Falls) and loud peals of thunder (Revelation 19:6).

What to make of all this singing? Craig Koester, New Testament professor at Luther Seminary, writes that "music plays a larger role in the book of Revelation than in any other book of the New Testament, and few books in all of Scripture have spawned more hymns sung in Christian worship today."[50] ("Holy, Holy, Holy"; "Let All Mortal Flesh Keep Silence and With Fear and Trembling Stand"; and of course, the graduation refrain "Hallelujah! Hallelujah.")

What to make of all this singing? Greg Carey, my New Testament faculty colleague, commented wryly to me recently about

---

49. Smith, "Songs of the Seer," 193.
50. Koester, "Distant Triumph Song," 243.

the frequent juxtaposition of these songs with conflict; and indeed, many of them are victory songs. Australian theologian and ethicist Robert S. Smith tells us these Revelation songs function in different ways: they create connections in the narrative, set the tone for certain scenes, do interpretive work, model celebration, encourage, and warn.[51] Dean of Duke Divinity Chapel Luke Powery believes these hymns, particularly the ones in Revelation 5, are a matrix of pain, praise, and politics within the historical setting of Roman oppression.[52] Powery informs us that "the hymns of Revelation show that proclaiming Jesus and God are essential for political engagement with the powers of the day, and to do otherwise is to fall prey to an anorexic theology of doxology."[53] You see, in John's vision it is Jesus and not Caesar who is celebrated as Lord. And *that* political statement will get you into trouble with Rome!

What to make of all this singing? While I agree with the observations of Koester, Carey, Smith, and Powery (multiple perspectives can be true at the same time), I have observations of my own. They come from my Africana cultural worldview that sees music as a cosmic life force with the power to shift the atmosphere, to transport the singer from one reality to another—from despair to hope. The public example of this uppermost in my mind is the moment in June 2015, when President Barack Obama began singing "Amazing Grace" at the funeral of Clementa Pinckney, the pastor of the AME church in Charleston, South Carolina, where nine people were killed by a visitor they had welcomed into their Bible study. Before Obama began singing, the air was tense and heavy with grief. No more than ten seconds into the hymn people were on their feet, tapping into that reservoir of goodness Obama had just been speaking about. The song shifted the atmosphere; it transported mourners into the grace-filled presence of the one who has borne their griefs and carried their sorrows.

This is the good news! This is how the prophet Habakkuk, in the midst of war and devastation can sing,

51. Smith, "Songs of the Seer," 197.
52. Powery, "Painful Praise," 69.
53. Powery, "Painful Praise," 76.

Preaching and Music

> Though the fig tree does not blossom and no fruit is on the vines; though the produce of the olive fails and the fields yield no food; though the flock is cut off from the fold and there is no herd in the stalls, yet I will rejoice in the LORD; I will exult in the God of my salvation. GOD the Lord is my strength; he makes my feet like the feet of a deer and makes me tread upon the heights. (Habakkuk 3:17–19)

These singing saints in Revelation know about hardship. They are the ones who have come out of the great ordeal. "For this reason [explains the elder to John] they are before the throne of God, and worship him day and night within his temple" (Revelation 9:14).

What to make of all this singing? Sometimes a song will carry you from here to there, from perplexity to peace, from weeping in the night to joy in the morning. The psalmists knew this when they sang, "Many are the afflictions of the righteous but the Lord delivers him out of them all" (Psalm 34:19). My enslaved ancestors knew this when they sang, "Sometimes I feel discouraged and think my work's in vain but then the Holy Spirit revives my soul again, there is a balm in Gilead to make the wounded whole. There is a balm in Gilead to heal the sin-sick soul."[54] "Isn't this escapism?" someone may ask. Not really. In my book this is more like soul care. Because life's hardships don't go away, but worship can restore our souls, giving us fresh energy to re-engage life's hardships. "What though my joys and comforts die? I know my Savior liveth. What though the darkness gather round? Songs in the night he giveth."[55]

It was the songs of Moses and Miriam that celebrated the journey of the Hebrews through that risky Red Sea passage from slavery to freedom; it was Mary's song that marked her transition from endangered pregnant teenager to bold servant of God; it was that song in the midst of hardship that transported Paul and Silas from incarceration to freedom. It was the songs of John and Charles Wesley that transported early Methodism from a sideshow gathering into a respected denomination. It was the freedom songs of the 1960s civil rights movement that kept hope alive in

---

54. "Balm in Gilead," Traditional, African American Spiritual.
55. Lowry, "My Life Flows On," 821.

the midst of law enforcement brutality and imprisonment. My siblings in Christ, it is often the songs of our faith that sustain us in the midst of hardship and escort us into the presence of God in worship. Ask Horatio Spafford, who wrote, "Whatever my lot thou hast taught me to say it is well, it is well with my soul."[56] This is the movement, the transition, the shift these singing saints who have come through the great ordeal in Revelation invite us into on this All Saints' Day.

A day of remembrance of loved ones who have died, some too soon, some too young, some too senselessly, it is this song of those who have come out of the great tribulation that enables us to see departed loved ones on a day like today. To imagine them singing in the presence of God where they will hunger no more, and thirst no more, where cancer will not strike them, nor any hate or war crime, nor any debilitating disease or addiction, for the Lamb at the center of the throne has escorted them across the threshold of death into a place where God will wipe away every tear from their eyes. These singing saints invite us into this means of grace, this shift from hardship to worship, from death to life.

> To God and to the Lamb I will sing, I will sing;
> to God and to the Lamb, I will sing.
> To God and to the Lamb who is the great "I AM,"
> while millions join the theme, I will sing, I will sing,
> while millions join the theme, I will sing.
>
> And when from death I'm free, I'll sing on, I'll sing on
> And when from death I'm free, I'll sing on
> And when from death I'm free, I'll sing and joyful be
> And through eternity, I'll sing on, I'll sing on
> And through eternity I'll sing on.[57]

May it be so. Amen.

---

56. Spafford, "It Is Well with My Soul," 840.
57. Anon., "What Wondrous Love Is This?"

5

Hymn Exegesis

THE WORK OF EXEGESIS is familiar to biblical scholars and seminary students. In preaching classes we do this work in order to analyze and explain the content and form of a select scripture text. Although the word "analysis" may also be used to describe what this chapter is about, I use the term "exegesis" to keep preaching and music in alignment with each other in the act of proclamation. When we exegete a biblical pericope we do a close reading and examination of the passage. We concern ourselves with matters of authorship, historical and cultural context, and the use of language—be that vocabulary, grammar, or idioms. We try to let the passage speak for itself. Our goal is to be as true as we can to the meaning it was originally intended to convey. I recommend a similar approach to a hymn or any congregational music that may be paired with a sermon. Just as a close reading of a biblical text can unearth understanding and meaning beyond what we hear or see on the surface, so too can a close reading of a congregational song reveal worth beyond the superficial or sentimental. Such exegesis may include at least seven areas of inquiry:

Hymn Exegesis

1. Biographical information on the author
2. The reason or occasion for writing the hymn
3. History of the hymn's use
4. Theological analysis
5. Literary analysis
6. Musical analysis
7. Homiletical analysis

Authorial information helps us understand the context out of which a song comes to us. The composer's faith story, when and where they lived, their educational background, musical influences, and other personal details of their lives all have some bearing on the content of a song. Denominational affiliation, gender, ethnicity, and similar identities are filters through which we interpret life and faith. As we would the authorship of any of the books in our biblical canon, in the same way we pay attention to the writers of the faith statements, prayers, and proclamations we sing on any given Sunday. Authorial information often gives us greater appreciation of what we sing; affinity of any kind with an author often deepens the value of a hymn for that particular singing community.

Occasional information provides background regarding why a particular song was written. Hymn stories are available in abundance. Besides books in print that curate and publish this information, there are blogs, articles, interviews, and other digitally available sources of these stories. Some online sources are virtual encyclopedias of this kind of information; see the appendix for a list of resources. Some of this information can be found as footnotes to the hymn in some hymnal editions, in cases where hymns have been commissioned for specific occasions or the author's words are cited in support of a particular hymn tune. Occasional information is important as it may provide a critical link between the hymn and the homily that deepens the impact of each.

Hymns, especially old ones, have a way of changing in the way they are used over time. The same holds true for biblical interpretation where the events of a historical moment may impact the use and meaning of a text. The way Hebrew scriptures are used by New Testament writers is an example of this. An old hymn such as "This Is My Father's World" may have been used at one time to reflect on the beauty of a morning walk.[1] Consider how that hymn may be used today to nudge a theologically conservative congregation toward being more aware of the impact our changing climate is having on "our Father's world." The hymnary.org website provides such information through the "Worship Notes" and "Bulletin Blurb" menu tabs in the "For Leaders"[2] section of their web page on the hymn. This historical information may not be available or even necessary for every hymn, but once in a while it may yield details that are significant for our congregational context.

Hymns often do theological reflection in the same way poems do existential or philosophical reflection, using words to examine or play with ideas. We have also established in chapter 1 that hymn writers are prone to wrestle with or at least reflect on scripture and theology in their lyrics. Charles Wesley's hymns, for example, are replete with biblical allusions and quotations as well as doctrinal statements; one biographer has called him a theological artist.[3] It can be both fun and enlightening to hold hymn lyrics up to theological examination. It is also necessary work for worship leaders committed to nurturing the theological formation of their congregations.

A hymn's literary analysis is helpful for making meaning of a hymn text, and it also holds great potential for a sermon. How many sermon titles have you heard that were either titles of or lyrical fragments of a song? Poets have ways of assembling words to strike the ear and land on the heart that contribute to the poem's persuasive impact. These words and phrases offer metaphors and imagery that appeal to a listener's sensory receptors. Unearthing these poetic devices is the work of literary analysis. When done

1. Babcock, "This Is My Father's World," in *Glory to God*, 370, footnote to hymn.

2. Babcock, "This Is My Father's World," Hymnary.org.

3. Rattenbury, *Evangelical Doctrines*, 86.

Hymn Exegesis

well it may even suggest to the preacher rhetorical strategies that make the sermon more compelling and memorable.

A musical analysis may be as nontechnical as asking the question, Does this tune convey appropriately the message of the hymn? This does not necessarily require musical training, just a set of aesthetic sensibilities that can tell whether the feel or mood of the melody matches the mood of the text. If the text conveys a sense of calm and rest, the tune should also feel calm and restful rather than agitated or excited. Another level of musical exegesis may require musical training or a keen musical ear, as one might ask how singable this hymn is. If there are too many words that outpace the mind's ability to think, it may either require some performance adaptation or the choice of another song altogether. If the melody spans a range of notes too wide for group singing, it may also require some performance adaptation—such as the combination of a lead singer and congregation—the use of another tune, or the choice of another song altogether.

A homiletical analysis of the hymn seeks to answer questions such as: What does this hymn proclaim? How does it proclaim this message? What are ways this song might be used in tandem with a sermon? In chapter 2 we talked about ways in which music may frame a sermon, either by orienting the listener to the sermon's main idea or by offering a way to respond to the sermon's invitation or challenge. Some hymns do homiletical work more explicitly and effectively than others; it is a gift when the preacher finds one that preaches well whether outside of the sermon proper or within the body of the preacher's delivery.

EXAMPLE—"RESTLESS WEAVER"

Not all these categories are necessary for an analysis of every hymn. However, these are important lenses to use when examining a hymn closely. One example is the hymn "Restless Weaver," by O. I. Cricket Harrison. This pen name gives no clue to the gender of the hymn writer. But a little online sleuthing turns up that she is Ola Irene Harrison, an ordained Disciples of Christ minister.

Preaching and Music

Professor Harrison "taught worship and church music at Lexington Theological Seminary and was on the development committee for the *Chalice Hymnal* and *Chalice Praise Hymnal* for the Disciples of Christ. She not only wrote hymns, but she also translated others' hymns into English."[4] This information about the author adds a degree of liturgical weight to the hymn, knowing that it came from someone with a love for and experience in church music, someone with an understanding of the proclamatory power of congregational song.

The inspiration for this hymn came to Harrison in 1988 as she attended a retreat held at a Catholic retreat center where the sisters who ran the center were weavers. In Harrison's words, "There were two working floor looms in the main conference hall. The community made hand-loomed hangings and blankets to help provide support. The theme of the retreat was 'Peace-ing it together' and the logo was a piecing quilt. So textiles, fabrics, textures were on my mind during the retreat."[5] This occasion was a gathering of congregations with a heart for peace and justice, generative themes for an idea that conjures the intertwining of spiritual values.

The hymn, written in 1988, was first published in the Disciples of Christ hymnal, for which Harrison was part of the editorial committee. It has also since been published in the *Upper Room Worshipbook* and the *Community of Christ Sings* hymnal. Set to the tune BEACH SPRING, its use has moved beyond congregational expression into arrangements for choirs and instrumental ensembles of all kinds. These multiple musical renditions offer a host of different ways to introduce this hymn to a congregation unfamiliar with it.

Theologically the hymn alludes to the feminine character of God. Although weaving is practiced by both men and women around the world, it is more commonly associated with the image of a woman at work. Biblically this picture of a deft Mother God alludes to the image used by the psalmist who writes, "You knit me together in my mother's womb" (Psalm 139:13 NRSV). The second

---

4. Clay, "Who or What is O. I. 'Cricket' Harrison?"
5. Wiener, "From 'Oh, My Father' to 'Restless Weaver.'"

verse foregrounds eco-theological themes with its mention of our urgent efforts at cleansing water, air, and land. This is both a prayer and a call for our stewardship of God's creation. Justice, peace, environmental activism, and a new world already and not yet are all woven into the stanzas of this hymn that is well suited to Earth Day and other times of ecological emphasis in worship. Singing this hymn reminds us that we are co-weavers with God's redemptive work in our world; it trains our eyes on that eschatological hope of God's reign on earth.

A close literary look will show trade words and imagery popping up through the fabric of this hymn. We find words such as ever-spinning, patterns, gathering up, fibers, texture, hue—all in verse one alone. The metaphor "earth's fragile web" is a poignant reference to the work of spiders whose delicately spun patterns bring to mind another kind of weaving: God weaves and God's creatures also weave. Each verse of this hymn turns the kaleidoscope, so to speak, giving us yet another striking image of this ever-spinning God, this Divine Restless Weaver.

The meter of the hymn, 8.7.8.7 D, makes it adaptable to several hymn tunes. It may be sung to HYMN TO JOY; this moves in a steady, majestic mode, which feels stable and grounded. BEACH SPRING is another, the one used in the *Chalice Hymnal*. In *Community of Christ Sings* it is set to the folk tune JEFFERSON. But I believe "Restless Weaver" works especially well with HOLY MANNA, because of the way this melody moves so restlessly up and down the musical scale, supporting and reinforcing the constant motion of a weaver at the loom and the animated movement of the loom itself. HOLY MANNA is the tune used in *The Upper Room Worshipbook*.

"Restless Weaver" is a fine example of proclamation in song. Although addressed to God in prayer-like fashion, it is a public prayer appropriate for worship. And in much the same way that the Lord's Prayer teaches us about prayer while it simultaneously proclaims the nature of the one to whom we pray, this hymn does more than simply petition God. It is a bold, explicit, corporate prayer—note the first-person plural pronouns—that informs us, heightens our awareness of God's dream, inspires and invites us to lean into that reign both as threads in its fabric and as co-weavers with God. Ultimately, "Restless Weaver" proclaims much about the nature of God and the nature of our work as people of God, weaving God's world anew.[6] This text may be used in tandem with any of several sermonic themes: social justice, international peace, climate justice or Earth Day, the kingdom or reign of God, or Christian vocation. The hymn also lends itself to numerous visual images that may be displayed on a screen during a sermon, an excellent way to deepen understanding and increase the sermon's impact and memorability.

> Restless Weaver, ever spinning threads of justice and shalom;
> Dreaming patterns of creation where all creatures find a home;
> Gathering up life's varied fibers, every texture, every hue:
> Grant us your creative vision. With us weave your world anew.
>
> Where earth's fragile web is raveling, help us mend each broken strand.
> Bless our urgent, bold endeavors cleansing water, air, and land.
> Through the Spirit's inspiration, off'ring health where once was pain,
> Strengthen us to be the stewards of your world knit whole again.
>
> When our violent lust for power ends in lives abused and torn,
> From compassion's sturdy fabric fashion hope and trust reborn.
> Where injustice rules as tyrant, give us courage, God, to dare
> Live our dreams of transformation. Make our lives incarnate prayer.
>
> Restless Weaver, still conceiving new life—now and yet to be,
> Binding all your vast creation in one living tapestry:
> You have called us to be weavers. Let your love guide all we do.
> With your Reign of Peace our pattern, we will weave your world anew.[7]

---

6. Wiener, "From 'Oh My Father' to 'Restless Weaver.'"
7. Harrison, "Restless Weaver." Used with permission.

Hymn Exegesis

PASTOR-MUSICIAN TALKING POINTS

The seven suggested areas of inquiry cover some branches of knowledge more easily accessible to trained or experienced musicians and some more readily accessible to pastors trained in theology and biblical studies. But most of the research—author's bio, occasion for writing, history of use, and literary features—can be done by both pastor and musician. A hymn analysis project has the potential to bring these two minds and leadership roles together in meaningful, purposeful dialogue. Consider this an opportunity for cross-training and learning together, an opportunity for rich conversation that expands each other's liturgical bandwidth. When this kind of in-depth study is done for one or two hymns related to the preaching moment in the service, it can increase the impact of the sermon while deepening the congregational experience of the music. But I invite you to consider another opportunity for featuring this kind of preaching that teaches and music that preaches: the hymn sing.

The nomenclature for this event in the *Canterbury Dictionary of Hymnology* is a hymn festival, which is on a slightly grander scale than the congregational hymn sing of this discussion, but it describes the event well:

> A hymn festival is a planned musical event where the singing of hymns is the primary activity used by a gathered community to worship and/or sing together. The selected hymns usually follow a designated theme and are interspersed with related readings, reflections, or prayers. Past hymn festival designs have been inspired by many topics, including the introduction of a new hymnal, a celebration of the Church's song, recognition of a hymn writer or church musician, an historic creed or text, and seasons of the Church year.[8]

This can be one of the most enjoyable partnerships of preaching and music, where pastor and musician bring out the best in each other. A well-planned hymn sing provides teaching and

---

8. Luhrs, "Hymn Festivals."

learning opportunities that have lasting impact due to the embodied nature of the experience. It allows hymns to preach in their own eloquent, poetic way. It allows for homiletical reflections that elevate the theological value of congregational songs. And it helps singers make strong associations between the music they sing and the way they live out their faith. Planned collaboratively by pastor and musician, this occasion brings out the teacher in each of these leaders. Just as teachers plan lessons with a goal, pastor and musician can prepare a hymn sing with a theme. Just as teachers determine what outcome they would hope to achieve by the end of the lesson, so pastor and musician can determine what they hope would result from this experience. And just as teachers decide on activities that would lead to the desired outcome, so pastor and musician can choose hymns and ways of singing them that could accomplish those goals.

I see this kind of collaboration as a way to build and strengthen the relationship between these two spiritual leaders. If the pastor is the one who chooses the Sunday hymns, this is an opportunity to discuss his or her selection criteria and process. The same holds true if the musician is the one who typically chooses the hymns; collaborative selection for a hymn sing can open up conversation around values and methods where beautiful cross-pollination and increased understanding happens. It is also a place for sharing their own perspectives of the congregation's musical tastes and history. What music has formed this congregation's theology? Where are the gaps that might be filled through informed singing such as a hymn sing could provide? What latent talents and skills among the people can be awakened through this event? Sharing along these lines can create what Westermeyer calls a "dialogue of grace," in which agreements and disagreements can lead to "a powerful partnership, which helps us all worship God in spirit and truth."[9]

---

9. Westermeyer, *Church Musician*, 102.

CONCLUSION

This partnership of preaching and music acknowledges, with gratitude, the integrity of hymn- and songwriters who thoughtfully align themselves with Scripture in crafting their lyrics. It also acknowledges the deep theological reflection many of these writers engage in their music, inviting us to do the same as we sing. Maybe this analytical look at hymns has inspired a reader to try their hand at writing their own hymn lyrics set to a well-known tune. I would encourage the reader to follow that impulse; it may turn out to be an important spiritual practice in the course of sermon preparation.

Epilogue

I BEGAN THIS BOOK with a prayer that music would take her place in and around the pulpit as a trustworthy proclaimer of the Word of God. The vision behind this prayer includes a deepened respect for music's value, beyond sentiment and artistry, beyond something to fill time or to facilitate liturgical transitions, beyond a canon of comfort or a trip down memory lane. I envision the music in our liturgy being taken seriously as a place where the voice of God is heard and the collective voice of the people responds. While the basic practice of combining preaching and music may be familiar to many, specific variations of this practice may not be as familiar. It is my hope that each of these chapters has prompted the preacher and music minister to take a deeper look at what they do in their ecclesial roles. May the synergy of their work, and that of preaching and music, amplify our proclamation of the good news of God "to accomplish abundantly far more than all we can ask or imagine."[1]

1. Ephesians 3:20 NRSVue.

Preaching and Music

God of sound and spheres,
tune our hearts to the frequencies of your grace and truth
as we proclaim your goodness and mercy,
your peace, joy and love,
your strength made perfect in weakness,
your pursuit of the lost,
your lifting up of the downtrodden,
your desire for justice and righteousness,
your abiding presence with us.
For the gift of proclamation in its many and various ways,
we give you thanks.
For songwriters who inspire our praise
eloquent and earthy,
we give you thanks.
For the blessed, holy conjoining of preaching and music
in its many-splendored ways,
we give you thanks.
Amen.

Appendix

ONLINE RESOURCES RELATED TO selection and research of congregational music:

- Hymnary.org: A free, robust site for searching hymns and songs with the help of several index features.
- Zeteosearch.org: A free, ecumenical resource with a search engine that pulls from—and connects researchers to—hundreds of preaching and worship websites, including denomination-specific sites.
- UMCdiscipleship.org: A History of Hymns archive is nested in the worship planning menu on this site.
- Lectionary.library.vanderbilt.edu: A free source of lectionary-related liturgical material, including art, music, and slideshows.
- Theafricanamericanlectionary.org: No longer live but has a good collection of archived material that highlights African American church traditions.

Appendix

- Congregationalsong.org: The resource and outreach arm of The Hymn Society of the United States and Canada.
- Worship.calvin.edu: Home of the Calvin Institute of Christian Worship, it hosts an array of bilingual print and digital resources.
- Carolynshymns.com: Home to the congregational music composed by Carolyn Winfrey Gillette. Gillette is known for writing hymns on new, contemporary subjects set to classic and familiar tunes.
- Songselect.ccli.com: A paid subscription to a copyright agency. Primarily songs in the praise and worship genre, but they are expanding their repertoire and search features.
- Onelicense.net: A paid subscription to a copyright agency with a robust selection of music. Lead sheets available.
- Themanyarehere.com: This "uncommon, intentionally diverse collective" writes congregational music with an indie pop and gospel sound. They are passionate about peace, justice, and inclusion.

Bibliography

Alexander, Cecil Frances. "Jesus Calls Us." In *Glory to God: The Presbyterian Hymnal*, edited by David Eicher, 720. Louisville: Westminster John Knox, 2013.

Allen, Lisa M. *The OneWord Worship Model: A New Paradigm for Church Worship Planning*. Eugene, OR: Cascade, 2023.

Anonymous. "How Can I Keep From Singing." Hymnary.org, n.d. https://hymnary.org/text/my_life_flows_on_in_endless_song_above.

Anonymous. "Pues Si Vivimos." Translated by Elise Eslinger. In *United Methodist Hymnal*, 356. Nashville: United Methodist Publishing House, 2009.

Anonymous. "What Wondrous Love Is This?" In *United Methodist Hymnal*, 292. Nashville: United Methodist Publishing House, 2009.

A. T. "The Framing of Pictures." *The Art Amateur* 12.4 (1885) 90. http://www.jstor.org/stable/25628307.

Babcock, Maltbie D. "This Is My Father's World." In *Glory to God: The Presbyterian Hymnal*, edited by David Eicher, 370. Louisville: Westminster John Knox, 2013.

———. "This Is My Father's World." Hymnary, n.d. https://hymnary.org/text/this_is_my_fathers_world_and_to_my.

Bell, John L. *The Singing Thing: A Case for Congregational Song*. Chicago: GIA, 2000.

Bibliography

———. "The Summons." In *Upper Room Worshipbook: Music and Liturgies for Spiritual Formation*, edited by Elise S. Eslinger, 60. Nashville: Upper Room, 2006.

Bombardo, John. "When All Else Fails, Preach a Hymn (But Not Any Hymn)." 1517: Christ for You, Sept. 18, 2022. https://www.1517.org/articles/when-all-else-fails-preach-a-hymn-but-not-any-hymn.

Bon Jovi, Jon, and Richard Sambora. "Who Says You Can't Go Home." On *Lost Highway*. Universal Music, 2007. https://lyrics.lyricfind.com/lyrics/bon-jovi-who-says-you-cant-go-home-2.

Borger, Joyce, Martin Tel, and John Witvliet, eds. *Psalms for All Seasons: A Complete Psalter for Worship*. Grand Rapids: Faith Alive Christian Resources, 2012.

Bringle, Mary Louise. "When Memory Fades." In *Glory to God: The Presbyterian Hymnal*, edited by David Eicher, 808. Louisville: Westminster John Knox, 2013.

Brown, Andrea. "The Power of Giving." Grandview Church Lancaster, 9:00 a.m. service, YouTube video, 28:30. Oct. 9, 2022. https://www.youtube.com/watch?v=CB5FobYitVE.

Brown, Sally A., and Luke A. Powery. *Ways of the Word: Learning to Preach for Your Time and Place*. Minneapolis: Fortress, 2016.

Brown, Teresa Fry. *Delivering the Sermon: Voice, Body, and Animation in Proclamation*. Minneapolis: Fortress, 2008.

Brueggemann, Walter. *Finally Comes the Poet: Daring Speech for Proclamation*. Minneapolis: Fortress, 1989.

Burnim, Melonee V., and Portia K. Maultsby. *African American Music: An Introduction*. New York: Routledge, Taylor & Francis, 2006.

Buttrick, David G. *Homiletic: Moves and Structures*. Minneapolis: Fortress, 1987.

Caesar, Shirley. *The Lady, the Melody, and the Word: The Shirley Caesar Story*. Nashville: Thomas Nelson, 1998. Kindle.

———. "Shirley Caesar: Tiny Desk (Home) Concert." NPR Music, YouTube video, 13:11. Feb. 25, 2022. https://www.youtube.com/watch?v=p3wLRo9zE5w.

Carlson, Dosia. "We Yearn, O Christ, for Wholeness." In *The New Century Hymnal*, edited by James W. Crawford, 179. Cleveland: Pilgrim, 1995.

"Cecil Frances Alexander." *The Canterbury Dictionary of Hymnology*. Canterbury Press, n.d. http://www.hymnology.co.uk/c/cecil-frances-alexander.

Cherry, Constance M. *The Worship Architect: A Blueprint for Designing Culturally Relevant and Biblically Faithful Services*. 2nd ed. Grand Rapids: Baker Academic, 2021.

Childers, Jana, and Clayton Schmit, eds. *Performance in Preaching*. Grand Rapids: Baker Academic, 2008.

Clay, Leslie. "Who or What Is O. I. 'Cricket' Harrison?" *Sisters in Song: Women Hymn Writers* (blog), June 2, 2014. https://sistersinsongwhw.wordpress.com/2014/06/02/who-or-what-is-o-i-cricket-harrison/.

Bibliography

Columba. "Christ Is the World's Redeemer." Translated by Duncan MacGregor, 1897. https://hymnary.org/text/christ_is_the_worlds_redeemer.

Cooney, Rory. "Canticle of the Turning." In *Upper Room Worshipbook: Music and Liturgies for Spiritual Formation*, edited by Elise S. Eslinger, 18. Nashville: Upper Room, 2006.

Costen, Melva Wilson. *African American Christian Worship*. 2nd ed. Nashville: Abingdon, 2007.

———. *In Spirit and in Truth: The Music of African American Worship*. Louisville: Westminster John Knox, 2004.

Crawford, Evans. *The Hum: Call and Response in African American Preaching*. Nashville: Abingdon, 1995.

Crawley, Ashon T. *Blackpentecostal Breath: The Aesthetics of Possibility*. New York: Fordham University Press, 2017.

Duck, Ruth. "God, We Thank You for Our People." In *The New Century Hymnal*, edited by James W. Crawford, 376. Cleveland: Pilgrim, 1995.

———. "When We Must Bear Persistent Pain." In *Glory to God: The Presbyterian Hymnal*, edited by David Eicher, 807. Louisville: Westminster John Knox, 2013.

———. *Worship for the Whole People of God*. 2nd ed. Louisville: Westminster John Knox, 2021.

Dutton, Jane. "Love Lingering." Grandview Church Lancaster, 9:00 a.m. service. YouTube video, 29:32. Oct. 30, 2022. https://www.youtube.com/watch?v=zMjJCBgYBAM.

The Editors of Encyclopedia Britannica. "St. Columba." *Encyclopedia Britannica*, Feb. 23, 2024. https://www.britannica.com/biography/Saint-Columba.

Faber, Frederick W. "There's a Wideness in God's Mercy." In *United Methodist Hymnal: Book of United Methodist Worship*, 121. Nashville: The United Methodist Publishing House, 2009.

Farrell, Bernadette. "Christ Be Our Light." In *Upper Room Worshipbook: Music and Liturgies for Spiritual Formation*, edited by Elise S. Eslinger, 114. Nashville: Upper Room, 2006.

Floyd, Samuel A., Jr. *The Power of Black Music: Interpreting Its History from Africa to the United States*. New York: Oxford University Press, 1995.

Gardner, Howard. *Frames of Mind: The Theory of Multiple Intelligences*. 10th anniversary ed. New York: Basic, 1993.

Geneva Academy of International Humanitarian Law and Human Rights. "Today's Armed Conflicts." n.d. https://geneva-academy.ch/galleries/today-s-armed-conflicts.

Gilbert, Kenyatta R. *The Journey and Promise of African American Preaching*. Minneapolis: Fortress, 2011.

Gilkes, Cheryl Townsend. "Shirley Caesar and the Souls of Black Folk: Gospel Music as Cultural Narrative and Critique." *The African American Pulpit* 6.2 (Spring 2003) 12–16.

Bibliography

Gillette, Carolyn Winfrey. "Hymns by Carolyn Winfrey Gillette." Carolyn's Hymns, Topical Index, n.d. https://www.carolynshymns.com/topical_index.html.

González, Justo L., and Pablo A. Jiménez. *Púlpito: An Introduction to Hispanic Preaching*. Nashville: Abingdon, 2005.

Greenhaw, David M., and Ronald J. Allen, eds. *Preaching in the Context of Worship*. St. Louis: Chalice, 2000.

Hale, Thomas A. *Griots and Griottes*. Bloomington: Indiana University Press, 1998.

Harrison, O. I. Cricket. "Restless Weaver." In *Upper Room Worshipbook: Music and Liturgies for Spiritual Formation*, edited by Elise S. Eslinger, 81. Nashville: Upper Room, 2006.

Haugen, Marty. "Gather Us In." In *Upper Room Worshipbook: Music and Liturgies for Spiritual Formation*, edited by Elise S. Eslinger, 54. Nashville: Upper Room, 2006.

Hawn, C. Michael. "History of Hymns: Jesus Calls Us O'er the Tumult." Discipleship Ministries, The United Methodist Church, Feb. 10, 2021. https://www.umcdiscipleship.org/articles/history-of-hymns-jesus-calls-us-oer-the-tumult.

———. "History of Hymns: What a Friend We Have in Jesus." Discipleship Ministries, The United Methodist Church, Feb. 3, 2021. https://www.umcdiscipleship.org/articles/history-of-hymns-what-a-friend-we-have-in-jesus.

Haynes, Frederick D., III. "And If You Don't Know, Now You Know." Eastern Star Church, YouTube video, 45:45. Oct. 25, 2023. https://www.youtube.com/watch?v=2lA1RPFYFwI.

Houston, Joel, Matt Crocker, and Salomon Lighthelm. "Oceans (Where Feet May Fail)." On *Zion*, 2013. Capitol CMG Publishing. https://lyrics.lyricfind.com/lyrics/hillsong-united-oceans-where-feet-may-fail-2.

Jay-Z. "Most Kingz." Track 5 on *Invasion Radio 2k10*. Produced by DJ Green Lantern, 2010.

Johnson, J. Rosamund, and James Weldon Johnson. *Lift Every Voice and Sing*. New York: E. B. Marks Music, 1921.

Johnson, James Weldon. *God's Trombones: Seven Negro Sermons in Verse*. New York: Penguin, 2008.

Joncas, Michael. "On Eagle's Wings." In *United Methodist Hymnal*, 143. Nashville: United Methodist Publishing House, 2009.

Jones, Alisha Lola. *Flaming? The Peculiar Theopolitics of Fire and Desire in Black Male Gospel Performance*. New York: Oxford University Press, 2020.

Jones, Kirk Byron. *The Jazz of Preaching: How to Preach with Great Freedom and Joy*. Nashville: Abingdon, 2004.

Jones, Lewis E. "There Is Power in the Blood." In *African American Heritage Hymnal*, 258. Chicago: GIA, 2001.

Kaan, Fred. "Help Us Accept Each Other." In *United Methodist Hymnal*, 560. Nashville: United Methodist Publishing House, 2009.

Bibliography

Kay, James F. *Preaching and Theology.* Missouri: Chalice, 2007.
Kimbrough, S. T. "Hymns Are Theology." *Theology Today* 42.1 (1985) 59–68.
King, Martin Luther, Jr. "MLK: I've Been to the Mountaintop!" The Martin Luther King, Jr. Center for Nonviolent Social Change, YouTube video, 43:14. Aug. 19, 2015. https://www.youtube.com/watch?v=gC6qxf3b3FI.
Koester, Craig R. "The Distant Triumph Song: Music and the Book of Revelation." *Word and World* 12.3 (1992) 243–49.
Kolb, Robert A. "Preaching on Luther's Hymn Texts in the Late Reformation." *Lutheran Quarterly* 34.1 (2020) 1–23.
Larson, Jonathan D. "Seasons of Love." On *Jonathan Sings Larson*, 2006. PS Classics. https://www.musixmatch.com/lyrics/Jonathan-Larson/Seasons-of-Love.
LaRue, Cleophus J. *The Heart of Black Preaching.* Louisville: Westminster John Knox, 2000.
———. *I Believe I'll Testify: The Art of African American Preaching.* Louisville: Westminster John Knox, 2011.
———, ed. *Power in the Pulpit: How America's Most Effective Black Preachers Prepare Their Sermons.* Louisville: Westminster John Knox, 2002.
Lischer, Richard. *The Preacher King: Martin Luther King, Jr. and the Word That Moved America.* New York: Oxford University Press, 1995.
Liu, Gerald C., and Khalia J. Williams. *A Worship Workbook: A Practical Guide for Extraordinary Liturgy.* Nashville: Abingdon, 2021.
Long, Thomas G. *Accompany Them with Singing: The Christian Funeral.* Louisville: Westminster John Knox, 2009.
———. *The Witness of Preaching.* 2nd ed. Louisville: Westminster John Knox, 2005.
Lowry, Robert. "My Life Flows On." In *Glory to God: The Presbyterian Hymnal*, edited by David Eicher, 821. Louisville: Westminster John Knox, 2013.
Luhrs, Ryan. "Hymn Festivals." *The Canterbury Dictionary of Hymnology.* Canterbury Press, n.d. http://www.hymnology.co.uk/h/hymn-festivals.
Maher, Matt. "Your Grace Is Enough." In *Lift Up Your Hearts: Psalms, Hymns, and Spiritual Songs*, edited by Joyce Borger et al., 698. Grand Rapids: Faith Alive Christian Resources, 2013.
McAllister, Pam. "What Hymn of Discipleship Challenges Consumerism?" *Ask Her About Hymn(s)* (blog), Apr. 26, 2018. https://askherabouthymn.com/what-hymn-of-discipleship-challenges-consumerism/.
Medema, Ken. "Lord Listen to Your Children Praying." In *Glory to God: The Presbyterian Hymnal*, edited by David Eicher, 469. Louisville: Westminster John Knox, 2013.
Menakem, Resmaa. *My Grandmother's Hands: Racialized Trauma and the Pathway to Mending Our Hearts and Bodies.* Las Vegas: Central Recovery, 2017.
Miller, Barbara Day. *The New Pastor's Guide to Leading Worship.* Nashville: Abingdon, 2006.

Bibliography

Newport, Kenneth G. C. *The Sermons of Charles Wesley*. New York: Oxford University Press, 2001.
Newton, John. "Amazing Grace." In *United Methodist Hymnal*, 378. Nashville: United Methodist Publishing, 2009.
"On the Framing of Pictures." *The Art Journal (1875–1887)* 6 (1880) 162–63. http://www.jstor.org/stable/20569525.
Peacey, John R. "Go Forth for God." In *United Methodist Hymnal*, 670. Nashville: United Methodist Publishing House, 2009.
Pew Research Center. "Why Americans Go (and Don't Go) to Religious Services." Aug. 1, 2018. https://www.pewresearch.org/religion/2018/08/01/why-americans-go-to-religious-services/.
Powery, Luke A. *Dem Dry Bones: Preaching, Death, and Hope*. Minneapolis: Fortress, 2012.
———. "Painful Praise: Exploring the Public Proclamation of the Hymns of Revelation." *Theology Today* 70.1 (2013) 69–78.
Proctor, Samuel D. *The Certain Sound of the Trumpet: Crafting a Sermon of Authority*. Valley Forge, PA: Judson, 1994.
Raboteau, Albert J. *A Fire in the Bones: Reflections on African-American Religious History*. Boston: Beacon, 1995.
Rambo, Shelly. *Spirit and Trauma: A Theology of Remaining*. Louisville: Westminster John Knox, 2010.
Ramshaw, Gail. *Christian Worship: 100,000 Sundays of Symbols and Rituals*. Minnesota: Fortress, 2009.
Rattenbury, J. Ernest. *The Evangelical Doctrines of Charles Wesley's Hymns*. 3rd ed. London: Epworth, 1954.
Redman, Matt, and Jonas Myrin. "10,000 Reasons." In *Lift Up Your Hearts: Psalms, Hymns, and Spiritual Songs*, edited by Joyce Borger et al., 559. Grand Rapids: Faith Alive Christian Resources, 2013.
Robinson, Robert. "Come Thou Fount." In *United Methodist Hymnal*, 400. Nashville: United Methodist Publishing House, 2009.
Rosenberg, Bruce A. *Can These Bones Live? The Art of the American Folk Preacher*. Rev. ed. Chicago: University of Illinois Press, 1988.
Schalk, Carl. "In Many and Various Ways, God Speaks." *Cross Accent* 15.1 (2016) 12–19.
Scheer, Greg. "People of the Lord." In *Glory to God: The Presbyterian Hymnal*, edited by David Eicher, 632. Louisville: Westminster John Knox, 2013.
Shelley, Braxton D. *Healing for the Soul: Richard Smallwood, the Vamp, and the Gospel Imagination*. New York: Oxford University Press, 2021.
Simmons, Martha, and Frank Thomas. *Preaching with Sacred Fire: An Anthology of African American Sermons 1750 to the Present*. New York: Norton, 2010.
Smith, Christine M. *Weaving the Sermon: Preaching in a Feminist Perspective*. Louisville: Westminster John Knox, 1989.
Smith, Robert S. "Songs of the Seer: The Purpose of Revelation's Hymns." *Themelios* 43.2 (2018) 193–204.

Bibliography

Sooter, Jacob, and Mia Fieldes. "Spirit of the Living God." On *Church Songs*, 2015. Vertical Church Band. https://www.musixmatch.com/lyrics/Vertical-Church-Band/Spirit-of-the-Living-God.

Spafford, Horatio G. "It Is Well with My Soul." In *Glory to God: The Presbyterian Hymnal*, edited by David Eicher, 840. Louisville: Westminster John Knox, 2013.

Spencer, Jon Michael. *Sacred Symphony: The Chanted Sermon of the Black Preacher*. Westport, CT: Greenwood, 1987.

"Spoken Word." Poetry Foundation: Glossary of Poetic Terms, n.d. https://www.poetryfoundation.org/learn/glossary-terms/spoken-word.

Stewart, Gina. "An Uncompromised Commitment." Christian Theological Seminary, YouTube video, 24:11. Feb. 4, 2015. https://www.youtube.com/watch?v=47dxoffCdSM.

Taizé Community. "Come and Fill Our Hearts." In *Glory to God: the Presbyterian Hymnal*, edited by David Eicher, 466. Louisville: Presbyterian Publishing, 2013.

Thomas, Frank A. *They Like to Never Quit Praisin' God: The Role of Celebration in Preaching*. Revised and updated. Cleveland: Pilgrim, 2013.

Thompson, Lindy. "I Do, in Fact, Go to Sing." *Hymn: A Journal of Congregational Song* 75.1 (2024) 34–35.

———. "I Go to Sing." *Lindy Thompson: Thoughts on the Spiritual Journey* (blog), Jan. 4, 2019. https://lindythompson.net/2019/01/04/i-go-to-sing/.

Thurman, Howard. *Deep River and the Negro Spiritual Speaks of Life and Death*. Richmond, IN: Friends United, 1990.

Troeger, Thomas H. "Silence! Frenzied, Unclean Spirit." In *Glory to God: The Presbyterian Hymnal*, edited by David Eicher, 181. Louisville: Westminster John Knox, 2013.

———. "Silence! Frenzied, Unclean Spirit." In *New Century Hymnal*, edited by James W. Crawford, 176. Cleveland: Pilgrim, 1995.

———. "We Have the Strength to Lift and Bear." In *New Century Hymnal*, edited by James W. Crawford, 178. Cleveland: Pilgrim, 1995.

———. *Wonder Reborn: Creating Sermons on Hymns, Music, and Poetry*. New York: Oxford University Press, 2010.

Troeger, Thomas H., and Leonora Tubbs Tisdale. *A Sermon Workbook: Exercises in the Art and Craft of Preaching*. Nashville: Abingdon, 2013.

Wagner, Kimberly R. *Fractured Ground: Preaching in the Wake of Mass Trauma*. Louisville: Westminster John Knox, 2023.

Walker, Wyatt Tee. *The Soul of Black Worship: Preaching, Praying, Singing*. New York: Martin Luther King Press, 1994.

Watts, Isaac. "Let Children Hear the Mighty Deeds." Hymntime, n.d. http://www.hymntime.com/tch/htm/l/e/t/c/letchild.htm.

Weaver, J. Dudley, Jr. "The Woman Hiding in the Crowd." In *Glory to God: The Presbyterian Hymnal*, edited by David Eicher, 178. Louisville: Westminster John Knox, 2013.

Bibliography

Westermeyer, Paul. *The Church Musician*. Rev. ed. Minneapolis: Augsburg Fortress, 1997.

Wiener, Michelle. "From 'Oh, My Father' to 'Restless Weaver'—Ola Is the New Eliza!" *Rational Faiths: Keeping Mormonism Weird* (blog), Aug. 24, 2016. https://rationalfaiths.com/restless-weaver/.

Wilhelm II. "Lord Jesus Christ Be Present Now." In *Lift Up Your Hearts: Psalms, Hymns, and Spiritual Songs*, edited by Joyce Borger, 524. Translated by Catherine Winkworth. Grand Rapids: Faith Alive Christian Resources, 2013.

Williams, Catherine E. "Let Me Tell You Why You're Here." Sermon presented at Lancaster Theological Seminary, Lancaster, PA, August 12, 2023.

———. "Proclamation: Many and Various Ways." *Theology Today* 79.1 (2022) 10–16. https://doi.org/10.1177/00405736211065461.

Wilson, Paul Scott, ed. *The New Interpreter's Handbook of Preaching*. Nashville: Abingdon, 2008.

Wren, Brian. *Praying Twice: The Music and Words of Congregational Song*. Louisville: Westminster John Knox, 2000.

Subject Index

acoustics, 50, 52
Adams, Charles G., 53
African American history, 72, 105
African American spirituals, xviii, 98, 104
Alexander, Cecil Frances, 12, 13
alignment, xix, 3, 52, 56
Allen, Lisa, 2
altar call, xix, 39
antiphony, 59, 75, 76, 79, 82
attunement, xx, 50, 52–57, 71, 72, 77, 81, 82, 83, 84, 85

Bell, John, 46
benediction, 18, 25
Black gospel homiletics, 50, 58, 80, 81
Blue Christmas service, 99
Bringle, Mary Louise, 103, 104
Brown, Sally A., 6
Brown, Teresa Fry, 57
Brueggemann, Walter, viii,
Buttrick, David, 58,

cadence, 63–64
cadenza/finale, 67–69, 74
Caesar, Shirley, ix, 80–84
call and response, xiii, 25, 37, 47, 57, 59,

Carey, Greg, 114, 115
chant, 15, 16
chanted sermon, 51,
Cherry, Constance, 37
choirs, xix, 21, 25, 41, 47
Christmas, 44, 45
church musicians, xiii, xiv, xix, xx, 5, 9, 10, 18, 20, 48, 125
climate justice, 124
collaboration, 1, 17, 25, 26, 74, 111, 126
congregational care, 103. 109
congregational repertoire, 19, 26, 38, 46, 47, 56,
congregational trauma, 86, 87
copyright licensing, 19
crescendo, 60, 70, 71, 73
cultural memory, 57, 107
cyberhymnal, 96

Duck, Ruth, 3, 10, 26, 45

Earth Day, 123, 124
exegesis, 13, 30, 54, 118

finale, 67–69, 74, 75
Floyd, Samuel, 57
focus and function, 27, 30–39, 49
framing, ix, 26–49, 95

Subject Index

freedom songs, 116
funeral sermons/services, 99, 100, 108, 111, 115

Gilbert, Kenyatta, 51
Gillette, Carolyn Winfrey, 111, 132
global pandemic, xxi, 88, 89, 92, 94, 111
Gonzalez, Justo, 7
gospel music, 80–82

harmony, xiii, xviii, 2, 9, 17, 52, 57, 92
Harrison, Ola Irene, 121, 122
Haynes, III, Frederick Douglass, 50, 76–80
heart songs/hymns, 4, 26, 56, 100, 109
hip-hop, 77, 78
Holmes, Zan, 53
Holy Spirit, xvii, xix, 35, 53, 54, 71
homiletical theory, vii, 27, 30
homiletics, x, xiv, xv
    Black gospel and, 50, 80
    musicology and, 57, 58, 81
hymn/song of response, xix, 27, 40, 43
hymn sing/festival, 48, 125, 126
hymn lyrics/texts, xvii, 38, 48, 95, 127
hymn of preparation, xix, 27, 35
hymn of response/invitation, xix, 27, 38, 40
hymn stories, 96, 97, 119
hymn tune, 111, 119, 123
hymnary.org, 19, 96, 120
hymns that preach, 101–2, 126

improvisation, 56, 57, 61, 63, 66–67, 72, 74, 81, 82
indexes, 19, 34, 38, 39, 45, 48, 99
instruments, 52, 56, 59, 64, 65, 68, 83, 84
intonation, 57, 63, 65–66, 68

jazz, 66, 67, 100
Johnson, James Weldon 53, 55
Jones, Alisha Lola, 54
Jones, Kirk Byron, 67

Kay, James, 5, 7, 11–15
Kimbrough, S T, 22
King, Jr., Martin Luther, 61, 75, 77
Knight, Carolyn, 53
Koester, Craig, 114, 115
Kolb, Robert A., xvii

lament, xx, 23, 98–99, 107
LaRue, Cleophus, 53, 54, 69, 82
literary analysis/exegesis, 13, 119, 120, 123, 125
liturgy, xv, xix, 1–26, 43, 109, 129
Long, Thomas, 7, 27, 30, 35, 99
Longest Night service, 99
Luther, Martin, xvii, 9
lyrical theology, 22–24
lyrics, xvi, xvii, 12, 19, 20, 25, 34, 40, 42, 78, 79, 98
    hymn, 18, 76, 95–96, 102, 104, 111, 120, 127

melisma, 66
melody, viii, xviii, 47, 57, 63, 68, 96, 106, 121, 123
memorial services, 99, 111
Menakem, Resmaa, 90, 92
meter, 19, 44, 45, 48, 63–64, 123
midrashim, 22
Moody, D. L, xviii.
movements/moves, vii, 51, 69, 70, 123
    sermonic, 58, 60, 79, 97. 102
music and theology, 9
music theory, 51, 52, 64
musical analysis/exegesis, 119, 121
musical intelligence, 11
musical transitions, 97–98
musicology, x, xv, xx, 50, 57–58

Obama, Barack, 115

Subject Index

online resources, 19, 20, 22, 31, 96, 110, 111, 119, 120

pacing, 62
pastor-musician conversations, xiv, 22–25, 44–49, 83–84, 109–12, 125–26
pauses, 62–63, 75, 76, 80, 82, 106
percussive Movement, 65, 68, 76, 80
Peterson, Eugene, 15
pitch, 47, 51, 53, 65, 68, 70, 81
playlist, 27, 38, 46, 110
poetry, viii, xvi, 9, 21, 23, 44, 45, 61, 69, 95, 98
Powery, Luke, xviii, 107, 108, 115
praise and worship music, 19, 41, 98
prayer vigils, 99
Proctor, Samuel 31,
psalms, xvi, 23, 24, 61, 98–99

Rambo, Shelly, 90
Rattenbury, J. Ernest, xvii
repetition, 57, 61–62, 63, 68, 72, 81, 82, 97
resonance, x, xiv, 52, 54, 55, 56, 67, 79, 102, 106
"Restless Weaver" (Harrison), 121–24
rhythm, xviii, 51, 53, 57, 59, 61, 63, 64–65

Sankey, Ira D., xviii
Schalk, Carl, 9
Scheer, Greg, 3
Schmit, Clayton, 9, 10
scripture text, 25, 54, 59, 106, 113, 118
sermon preparation, 30, 53, 83, 127
sermonic selection, 35, 54
Shelley, Braxton D., 80
Simmons, Martha, 68
singing and health, 92
singing that preaches, 80–82, 99, 101–2

Smith, Christine, 103
Smith, Robert S., 115
social justice, 3, 16, 71, 124
solo pastors, 18–19, 21
song as proclamation, viii, xvii, 25, 28
Spafford, Horatio, 117
Spencer, Jon Michael, 57, 64
Spiritual tuning, 54, 72
Spirituals. *See* African American Spirituals
Stackhouse, Rochelle, 38
Stewart, Gina, 50, 69–76
synergy, xiii, xviii, 12, 27, 28, 35, 40, 53, 66, 129

Tel, Martin 4, 11
tempo, 58, 59, 62, 73, 76, 111
theme and variations, xviii
Thomas, Frank, 54, 56, 75
Thompson, Lindy, 92–94
Tiny Desk Concert, 80–82
trauma-informed preaching, 86–102
Troeger, Thomas, 11, 22, 97, 101, 102, 105, 106
tuning, 52–57
tuning up, 55, 56

vamp, 79, 81, 82
volume, 55, 60–61, 68,

Wagner, Kimberly, 89, 107
Walker, Wyatt Tee, 77
Watts, Isaac, 3
Weaver, J. Dudley, 101
Wesley, Charles, xvii, 116, 120
whooping, 66, 68
Wilson, Melva Costen, 6
Winans, Marvin, 80
word play, 64, 78
worship design, 4, 17–18, 89
worship planners/planning, xix, 1, 26, 29, 37, 47, 48, 49, 89
Wren, Brian, 48

Scripture Index

OLD TESTAMENT

Exodus
1:15–22	69
15:20–21	viii, xvi

1 Samuel
1:1–10	viii

Nehemiah
8:8	31

Psalms
19:4	11
22	23
31:5	23
34:19	116
78:1–8	3
103	20
139:13	122

Jeremiah
8:22	105

Habakkuk
3:17–19	116

Zephaniah
3:14–20	viii
3:17–18a	vii

NEW TESTAMENT

Matthew
4:18–20	41
5:13–16	15, 16

Mark
1:16–17	13
1:21–28	101

Luke
1:46–55	viii, 25
3:10	36
4:31–37	101
15:11–32	32

Scripture Index

John

1:1	vii
1:14	vii
1:35–42	13
18:1–11	77
21:15–19	41

Acts

2:37	36

Romans

8:30	63

Philippians

2:5–11	viii

Hebrews

1:1	8

Revelation

1:9	113
5:8–13	viii
7:9–17	112
9:14	116
19:6	114

Song Title Index

Amazing Grace, 34, 44, 115
At the Cross, 79
Away in a Manger, 44, 45

Backstabbers, 77
Balm in Gilead, 104, 105, 116
Black Rage, 78

Christ Be Our Light, 16
Christ is the World's Redeemer, 11
Come Thou Fount of Every Blessing, 40, 46
Coming Back, 39

Depth of Mercy, 39

For Unto Us a Child Is Born, 66

Gather Us In, 41, 42
Go Forth for God, 37
God, We Thank You for Our People, 3
Glory, Glory Hallelujah Since I Laid My Burden Down, 3, 79

Hallelujah Chorus, 66, 114
Have Thine Own Way, Lord, 77
Help Us Accept Each Other, 37
Holy, Holy, Holy, 114

How Firm a Foundation, 45

Immortal, Invisible, God Only Wise, 45
I Don't Feel No Ways Tired, 76
I Want Jesus to Walk with Me, 100
I've Got a Feeling Everything's Gonna Be Alright, 79
It Is Well with My Soul, 3, 47
It's A Man's World, 71
It's Alright, 82

Jesus Calls Us, 12
Jesus Paid It All, 79
Joy To the World, 44
Juicy, 77
Just As I Am, 39

Let Children Hear the Mighty Deeds, 3
Let There Be Peace on Earth, 3

My Soul Cries Out with a Joyful Shout, 25

O To Be Kept by Jesus, 77
Oceans, 41, 42
Ode To Joy, 58

Song Title Index

On Eagle's Wings, 47

Pues Si Vivimos, 41, 42

Restless Weaver, 121–24

Seasons of Love, 38–39
Silence! Frenzied, Unclean Spirit, 101
Spirt of the Living God, 41, 42
Stand By Me, 100

10,000 Reasons, 20
The Prayer, xiii
The Summons, 41, 43
The Woman Hiding in the Crowd, 101
There's a Wideness in God's Mercy, 34
Thank You for Hearing Me, 97
This Is My Father's World, 120
This Little Light of Mine, 17
Through It All, 100

Use Me Up, 39

We Have the Strength to Lift and Bear, 102
We Need to Hear from You, 77
We Shall Overcome Someday, 3
We Yearn, O Christ for Wholeness, 102
What A Friend We Have in Jesus, 96, 100
What We Have Heard, What We Have Known, 3
What Wondrous Love Is This? 99
When Memory Fades, 103, 104
When The Saints Go Marching In, 100
When We Must Bear Persistent Pain, 102
Who Says You Can't Go Home, 40
With Fear and Trembling Stand, 114

Your Grace is Enough, 34

www.ingramcontent.com/pod-product-compliance
Lightning Source LLC
Chambersburg PA
CBHW030857170426
43193CB00009BA/646